異國風味

越南菜

D1409718

VIETNAMESE CUISINE

蔡芝 Muoi Thai Loangkote

味全食譜
Wei-Chuan Cookbook

總 編 輯：黃淑惠
食譜提供：蔡芝
顧　　問：張雪玲

翻　　譯：陳美君、賴燕貞
文稿協助：詹麗莎、何久恩、林淑華、華茵、梁偉業、陳素真

攝　　影：大野現
設　　計：馬紀雯、張菲

電腦排版：友坤電腦排版有限公司
分色製版：大光華印務部
印　　刷：錦龍印刷實業股份有限公司

版權所有：局版台業字第 0179 號
　　　　　1999 年 10 月初版　1-0-8
　　　　　2003 年 9 月 4版　4-3-2

EDITOR: Su-Huei Huang
RECIPES: Muoi Thai Loangkote
CONSULTANT: Tuyet Linh Wong

TRANSLATION: Meghan Chen, Yen-Jen Lai
EDITORIAL STAFF: Lisa Jan, John Holt, Sophia Lin, Innie Hua,
Jarrod Leung

PHOTOGRAPHY: Aki Ohno
DESIGM: Yvette Ma, Faye Chang

PRINTED IN TAIWAN

WEI-CHUAN PUBLISHING
1445 Monterey Pass Rd., #110
Monterey Park, CA 91754, USA.
Tel: (323) 261 · 3880
Fax: (323) 261· 3299
www.weichuancookbook.com
wc@weichuancookbook.com

FIRST PRINTING: OCTOBER 1999
FOURTH PRINTING: SEPTEMBER 2003

ISBN: 0-941676-77-3

7 16598 00077 2

目錄 · CONTENTS

序 越南菜融合了中國、泰國、寮國、馬來西亞等鄰近國家的飲食文化，再加上越南曾經是法國的殖民地，所以越南菜口味相當多元，一如越南文化集合了各文化的風華。

越南飲食的多元性，反映在多變化的用餐方式上，包括中式的三或四菜一湯；越式的簡餐如炒飯、炒麵和各式湯粉、檬[米粉]、麵等；西式的單一菜餚配麵包[如茄汁牛肉]及法式三明治演變而來的越式三明治。傳統的越南菜大多是用香草葉、香味配料、沾料及肉類互相搭配，並用米紙或生菜包食，或與檬拌食，其特性是不油膩且開胃，所搭配的各種香草葉俱食療價值，因此現代化的越南菜不僅變化多，也被視為一種健康菜餚，近年日益普遍，風行各地。

越南菜的沾料好壞影響菜餚美味，調製方法亦不盡相同，書內除了介紹我們家的獨特配方，以下幾點亦有助於認識及享用道地的越南菜：

- ≈ 為方便讀者，每道菜皆試做多次，力求材料及份量簡單正確。

- ≈ 書內大部份菜餚份量均是二人份的設計，擬定菜單時，可選一道海鮮或肉類，再加蔬菜及主食即可。

- ≈ 越南菜融合了多種國家的飲食菁華，食用時依情況用筷子、刀叉、或用手。

- ≈ 一般越南家庭，餐桌上均備有新鮮辣椒、辣椒醬、青檸檬、醋、魚露等，用餐時依自己口味添加。

我生於越南堤岸，從小就熱衷烹飪，在當地曾拜名師學習廚藝。 1980 年移居美國，由於在美國材料選購方便，且週圍的親友大部份來自越南，使我對越南菜的研究更加得心應手，所以經常約親友到家中分享越南菜，也因此經友人的介紹，有機會與味全出版社合作編書。寫食譜不如在家做菜輕鬆，蒐集資料過程中，得到親友很多寶貴意見，在此表示謝意外，也感謝味全編輯組的大力幫忙，尤其是張雪玲老師的參與，使得本書內容更充實完美。張雪玲老師是生長在越南的華僑，國立台灣師範大學家政系畢業後，先後在台灣及香港擔任烹飪老師多年。最後也感謝外子，在這一段時間給予我支持與鼓勵。

Introduction

Vietnamese cuisine embodies the culinary influences of China, Thailand, Laos, Cambodia, and Malaysia. In addition, the influence from many years of French colonization has added to a unique blend of flavors to an already aromatic and exotic cuisine.

The many varieties of Vietnamese cuisine are reflected in the ways in which meals are served: the common Chinese meal of three or four dishes accompanied by soup; the Vietnamese one dish meal of fried rice or stir-fried noodles, various types of noodle soups and rice noodles; Western style meals include one dish meals served with bread (such as Beef in Tomato Sauce) and the Vietnamese sandwich which derived from the French version. Traditional Vietnamese cooking uses fragrant herbs/spices, fragrant accompaniments, dipping sauces, and meats to mix and match flavors; wrapped with rice paper or lettuce, or mixed with rice noodles and served. Such practices render Vietnamese food as not oily and uniquely light and appetizing. The various fragrant herbs and spices used are thought to have healing properties. Therefore, modern Vietnamese cuisine is not only colorful and varied, it is also perceived as a healthy cuisine. Hence it is becoming more popular everywhere.

Vietnamese dipping sauces can influence the flavor of any dish, since they may be made in very different ways. This book introduces several sauces, including our own special family recipe. Below are a few points to facilitate an understanding and appreciation of authentic Vietnamese cuisine:

- ≈ The reader is assured, every recipe was tested many times to ensure that ingredients and portions are simple and accurate.
- ≈ Most of the recipes serve two. When organizing a meal, you may select seafood or meat as the main dish, and add a vegetable dish to accompany.
- ≈ Because Vietnamese cuisine is comprised of many cultures, chopsticks, knives, and forks, or hands may be used according to the type of meals.
- ≈ In most Vietnamese homes, fresh chili pepper, chili paste, limes, vinegar, and fish sauce are permanent fixtures on the dining table and are used as desired on any dish.

I have loved cooking since I was a child in Vietnam and luckily was able to study under famous chefs. In 1980 I immigrated to the United States and discovered that ingredients for Vietnamese cooking were readily available. Accordingly, I was able to continue in my culinary research and practice.

In the process of collecting information, I gained a great deal of valuable insights and suggestions from Vietnamese friends and family to whom I am grateful. I also thank the tremendous support of the Wei-Chuan Publishing editorial staff, especially Ms. Tuyet Linh Wong's consultations, which contributed to the richness of this cookbook's content. Ms. Wong is an ethnic Chinese immigrant who was born and raised in Vietnam. After she graduated from National Taiwan Normal University with a degree in home economics, she taught for many years in Taiwan and later, in Hong Kong. Finally I thank my spouse who gave me support and encouragement while I wrote this cookbook.

Mui Thai Leongkute

量器介紹
MEASUREMENTS

本食譜是採用標準量器來設定調味份量，量調味品時宜裝滿，表面與量器齊平。

The following measuring tools are used in this book. When measuring ingredients, pour or fill into container until full, then level.

| 1 杯（1 飯碗）=16 大匙 | 1 大匙（1 湯匙） | 1 小匙（1 茶匙） |
| 1 cup (1 c.) = 236 c.c. | 1 Tablespoon (1 T.) = 15 c.c. | 1 teaspoon (1 t.) = 5 c.c. |

常用調味料及材料
FREQUENTLY USED SAUCES AND INGREDIENTS

魚露（圖 1）由魚提煉製成的調味品，味鹹、呈淡茶色，使用方法與醬油同。

醬油（圖 2）黃豆或黑豆蒸熟發酵後加鹽、水調製而成；有深色（老抽）、淡色（生抽）及一般三種，如無特別說明，就用一般醬油。

蠔油 生蠔發酵後加鹽水調製而成，具特殊海鮮美味，使用方法與醬油同。

紅醋（圖 3）又名"浙醋"，呈暗紅色，可使用在含膠質的湯羹或炒粉、麵及一些鹹點上，可助消化及減油膩。

酸子（圖 4）是一種天然植物的果實，果肉呈棕色，是菜餚中酸味來源之一。

Fish Sauce (Fig.1)   A salty fish extract of caramel color that functions like soy sauce.

Soy Sauce (Fig.2)   Made from fermented steamed soy or black beans, salt, and water. It comes in dark, light, and regular varieties. If not specified in recipes, use regular.

Oyster Sauce   Made from fermented oysters, salt, and water; is unique in its seafood flavor. It is used like soy sauce.

Red Rice Vinegar (Fig.3)   This burgundy hued flavoring agent may be used in any thickened broth, on stir-fried rice sheets or noodles, and other salty delicacies. It also can help digestion and reduce oiliness.

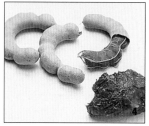

Tamarind (Fig.4)   A fruit with brown flesh that is a source of tartness and sourness.

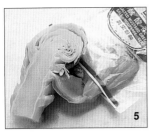

鹹酸菜（圖 5）是一種醃菜，買現成或自己做，大芥菜 2 斤 4 兩（1350 公克）洗淨，曬至八分乾，加 3 大匙鹽，搓軟，置 2 小時擠出鹽水後置玻璃罐內；加 5 杯冷開水及 3 大匙鹽，醃數天至菜變黃即可食用。如要快點變酸，可多加 1 大匙的糖，或 1 大匙粥水。剛做出來的新鹹酸菜清脆可口，味道不十分酸，但有一股辛辣嗆鼻的風味。鹹酸菜用途很多，可與其他材料炒、煮湯、涼拌或與其他菜餚配食，可增加食慾。鹹酸菜放入冰箱可置 2 個月。

辣椒醬（圖 6）可取代辣椒來調製"甜酸辣魚露沾料"或隨意加在菜餚內。

辣椒（圖 7）有新鮮和乾的。種類很多，辣的程度也不同，通常越小的辣椒越辣。辣椒除增加菜餚的色彩外，尚可刺激食慾。

香茅（圖 8）一種辛香料，有新鮮、切碎冷藏及晒乾的。用來做醃料、炒或煮。

南薑（圖 9）是薑的一種，有特殊的香味，可採用新鮮或乾的（乾的泡水即軟）。搗碎後加入菜餚內可增加香味，也可切塊置滷汁或湯內，可用薑取代。

蝦米（圖 10）即曬乾的蝦，使用前略洗或泡水，炒香加在菜餚內或熬湯，可增加鮮味。

生菜（圖 11）生菜可用來包捲菜餚，或切絲放入檬內，是越南菜內常用的蔬菜。

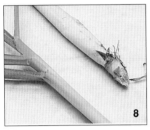

Pickled Mustard Cabbage (Fig.5) A type of pickled vegetable that may be purchased or homemade. If homemade, use 3 lbs. (1350g) mustard greens. Wash, then sun dry until 80% dry, add 3 tablespoon salt and rub into vegetable until soft. Set aside 2 hrs., squeeze out excess water, and place in a glass jar. Add 5 cups cold water and 3 tablespoon salt and marinate for several days until vegetable turns yellow, indicating readiness. If a quicker process is desired, add 1 tablespoon sugar or 1 tablespoon porridge water. Freshly made pickled vegetables are crunchy and create a sensation that is not too tart and yet gives the sinus a stingy rush. Pickled mustard greens have many uses: in stir-fry with other ingredients, in soups, salads, or other combinations to enhance flavor with the added benefit of improving appetite. May be refrigerated for up to two months.

Chili Paste (Fig.6) May substitute for chili to make "sweet/sour/spicy fish sauce" or added to any desired dish.

Chili Peppers (Fig.7) Available fresh or dried, many types with varying degrees of hotness. Usually the smaller the chilies, the more powerful the punch. Besides adding color to the dishes, chilies can stimulate appetite.

Lemon Grass (Fig.8) Sold fresh, chopped and refrigerated, or sun-dried. This spice may be used in pickling, stir-frying, or general cooking.

Galangal (Fig.9) A ginger variety with a special fragrance; may be used in fresh, or dried form after soaking. Crush and add to enliven flavor in dishes. May be used in simmering sauces and soups as a ginger substitute.

Dried Shrimp (Fig.10) Sun dried shrimp, used after rinsing lightly or soaking in water to make flavorful dishes and soups.

Lettuce (Fig.11) May be used to wrap food or shred to add to rice noodles. It is a commonly used vegetable in Vietnamese cooking.

香菇、木耳（圖 12）香菇是栽培在木頭上的菇類（右），木耳是生長在朽木上的菌類（左）使用前先泡軟，急用時可用熱水浸泡。

泰國檸檬葉（圖 13）即皺皮檸檬的樹葉，有奇特香味，煮湯、咖哩或炒菜時可用，也可加入魚漿或絞肉內做成肉餅。

法國香葉（圖 14）又稱玉桂葉，加入肉或海鮮類內煮，有去腥及增加香味的功用。

青檸檬（圖 15）青色檸檬無籽，又稱"萊姆"，熟透時皮會變黃，比黃色檸檬酸。一般越南菜均使用青檸檬，若無青檸檬可用白醋或黃色檸檬取代。

去皮綠豆（圖 16）即去殼的綠豆仁。蒸過的去皮綠豆用途很多，做法為去皮綠豆 1 杯泡水 4 小時，中間換水多次以去鹼味，瀝乾後，大火蒸 40 分鐘至豆軟即可。若用微波爐，上蓋濕紙巾，下面隔水加熱 10 分鐘，蒸後的份量為 2 杯。

椰汁、椰茸（圖 17）嫩的椰子稱青椰子（左），其椰汁可用來烹煮菜餚。罐裝椰汁糖份略高。老椰子外殼呈棕色（右），裏面肉厚，刨絲即成椰茸。

椰奶（圖 18）椰茸 1 杯加溫水 1½ 杯，用果汁機攪勻過濾，可製 1 杯椰奶，或用椰奶粉加水調製。也有現成罐裝及小盒包裝。椰奶不宜用大火加熱，加入椰奶的食物較易變質，宜食時才加。若無椰奶可用牛奶取代。

椰漿 椰奶 ¾ 杯加鹽 ⅛ 小匙，用小火邊攪煮至 ½ 杯濃汁。可加在甜點上。

Chinese Black Mushrooms, Dried Wood Ears (Fig.12) Black mushrooms are grown on wood (right) while wood ears are a fungus grown from dead wood (left). Both require soaking prior to use. When in a hurry, soak in hot water.

Kaffir Leaves (Fig.13) Leaves of the wrinkled lemon tree; a unique fragrance which adds a fine aroma to soups, curry, stir-fry, fish paste or ground meat patties.

Bay Leaves (Fig.14) Removes strong odors and enhances flavor of meat or seafood dishes.

Lime (Fig.15) Seedless and more tart than lemon; turns yellow when ripe. Usually lime is used in Vietnamese cooking. If lime is not available, white vinegar or lemon may be used.

Peeled Mung Beans (Fig.16) Are peeled green peas that offer multiple uses when steamed. To steam, soak 1 cup peeled green peas in water for 4 hours. Change the water often to reduce rawness of taste, drain then steam high for 40 minutes until soft. If using microwave oven, cover with wet paper towel and place on another bowl of water, steam 10 minutes. Yields 2 cups.

Coconut Juice, Coconut Shreds (Fig.17) Green coconuts are tender (left), the juice may be used for cooking. Canned juice has a higher sugar content. Brown coconuts are older (right), their flesh is thicker and more useful in making coconut shreds.

Coconut Milk (Fig.18) Add 1½ cups warm water to 1 cup coconut shreds. Mix thoroughly with a blender and strain, makes 1 cup coconut milk. Alternatively, may use coconut milk powder mixed with water or use canned or packaged milk. Do not use high heat to warm coconut milk. Since foods to which coconut milk is added tend to spoil easily, it is best used just before serving. If coconut milk is unavailable, regular milk may be substituted.

Thick Coconut Milk May be used to top desserts. To make, add ⅛ teaspoon salt to ¾ cup coconut milk, stir while cooking in low heat until it yields ½ cup thick milk.

19

20

21

22

23

24

25

印度咖哩籽(圖 19)可做紅油。油 2 大匙燒熱,用小火將咖哩籽炒香,油呈紅色,咖哩籽變黑即撈出。做好的紅油可增加菜餚的顏色。

冬粉(粉絲)(圖 20)綠豆粉製成的細條粉絲,使用前先泡水,煮後呈透明狀,可炒或加入湯內,加在餡料內有助吸乾餡料的水份。

Annatto Seeds (Fig.19) Produce red oil to add color to dishes. Heat 2 T. oil, use low heat and stir-fry annatto seeds until fragrant and the oil turns red. Remove the blackened seeds.

Bean Threads (Fig.20) Made from green pea powder, these thin, dry, off-white threads become translucent after cooking. Soak prior to use. May use in stir-fry or soups. Absorbs liquid when used as a filling inside dumplings.

高湯做法
STOCK

一般高湯　將雞腿或豬骨 1½ 斤(900 公克)切塊,先在滾水內川燙,再加 20 杯水煮滾後去除泡沫,改中火煮 2 小時至汁剩 10 杯即成高湯。煮時可隨意加入蝦米、乾干貝、冰凍或乾的淡菜或烤的魷魚(圖 21)等。每種材料各有不同的鮮味。做越南菜時,用高湯的機會很多,常準備一些高湯待用很方便。

牛高湯　牛尾 1½ 斤(900 公克)切塊,在滾水內川燙,薑一塊及洋蔥一個烤香後(圖 22),略洗去黑焦部份,連同 20 杯水、草果 3 粒(圖 23)、香菜籽 1 小匙(圖 24)、桂皮 1 小塊(圖 25)及茴香子(見 17 頁圖 2)1 小匙,去除泡沫,改用中火煮 2 小時至汁剩 10 杯即成。牛高湯可用在牛肉粉上(見 67 頁)。

Common Stock Cut 2 lbs. (900g) chicken legs or pork bones in pieces, and blanch in boiling water, discard used water. Add 20 cups water and boil, remove surface suds, reduce to medium heat and cook for 2 hrs. until liquid is reduced to 10 cups which becomes stock. If desired, may add dried shrimp, dried scallops, frozen or dried mussels or baked squid (Fig.21). Each type of ingredient adds a different flavor. Stock is used frequently in Vietnamese dishes; therefore preparing large quantities for future use lends to convenience.

Beef Stock Cut 2 lbs. (900g) beef tail into pieces, blanch in boiling water; bake until fragrant one piece of ginger root and one onion (Fig.22). Wash away the burnt parts, add to 20 cups of water, 3 kernels of fructus amomi (Fig.23), 1 t. coriander seeds (Fig.24), one small piece of cinnamon (Fig.25), and 1 t. fennel seeds (p.17, Fig.2) until boiling, remove foam. Reduce to medium heat and cook for two hours until 10 cups of stock remain. Beef stock may be used for beef rice noodle soup (see p.67).

越南人的主食
VIETNAMESE STAPLES

越南的飲食文化受中國、法國以及鄰近國家的影響，其主食除米、麵條、麵包外，還用米紙、檬(米粉)、河粉、粿條、瀨粉等。以下介紹一些較特殊的材料：

碎米 越南人除食用一般的米之外，也經常吃飯粒不黏的碎米飯。

米紙(圖1)即米漿製成的乾薄餅，以色白、沒裂痕者為佳，泡軟後用來包捲餡料(餡料置粗糙面上)。米紙有各種不同的尺寸，如使用大張的(直徑約30公分)，捲好菜餚後，可切段食用；小張的(直徑約15公分)用來現包現吃。使用前將米紙浸水放紙巾上，再鋪一張紙巾，如此疊放數層，待水份收乾呈濕軟即可。也可用整疊塑膠製專用盤子(圖2)，將20張米紙浸濕後夾入。急用時可浸熱水(不可太燙否則易破)。

檬(米粉)(圖3)檬可煮湯、淋甜酸辣魚露涼拌、也可放入米紙或生菜內包捲。新鮮的檬放入滾水內川燙即可用，乾檬因粗細而煮的時間不同。

煮粗條乾檬時，用20杯水燒開，放入檬8兩(300公克)，煮開立即熄火，蓋鍋燜14分鐘，粉心熟透即撈出，放入冷水中，等水變中溫時，一份份撈出盤捲後，盛在篩子內(圖3)，用時較方便，待水份收乾時即可用。

細條乾檬煮法相同，唯燜的時間減半。

最細的檬即台灣細米粉，一般用來製檳海，"檳海"做法見第59頁。

Vietnamese cuisine embodies influences by Chinese, French, and neighboring cultures. Besides rice, noodles made from flour, and bread, Vietnamese staples also include Banh Trang (rice paper), Bun (rice noodles), Banh Pho (fresh rice noodles), tapioca sticks, Vietnamese rice noodles, and other products made from rice. Below is an introduction to some unique ingredients:

Broken Jasmine Rice (Gao Tam) Vietnamese people use ordinary rice as well as ground, non-sticky rice.

Rice Paper (Banh Trang) (Fig.1) Dried paper thin sheets made from rice batter. Perfect white sheets without tears are ideal since they are used for wrapping. Soak before using. Place filling on the rough texture side. Rice paper comes in different sizes. When using larger ones (diameter 12", 30cm), may cut the wrapped flute into sections to serve. Small sheets (diameter 6", 15cm) are for wrapping and serving at the table. To soak, dip rice paper in water then place on a paper towel. Layer another sheet of paper towel on top of the rice paper. Repeat with additional layers of rice paper, interspersed with sheets of paper towel until excess water is absorbed and the rice paper is softened. May also use a stack of 20 special plastic plates for preparing rice paper (Fig.2), place one sheet soaked rice paper onto each plate. When in a hurry may use hot water, but not too hot since the rice paper may tear more easily.

Rice Noodles (Bun) (Fig.3) Used in soups, salads tossed with sweet/sour/spicy fish sauce, or as a filling in rice paper or lettuce wraps. Fresh rice noodles may be used after blanching in boiling water. Because dried rice noodles come in various thicknesses, cooking time varies. When cooking thick dried rice noodles, boil 20 cups water, and cook ⅔ lb. (300g) rice noodles until boiling. Shut off heat immediately and cover for 14 minutes. When noodles are cooked through, remove and soak in cold water until water becomes lukewarm. Remove a portion of noodles at a time and wrap around fingers then place all the portions in a strainer to drain (Fig.3), so that they are convenient to use. Serve when dry. Thin dried rice noodles are cooked the same way as their thicker counterpart, except the covered steamed time is half the time.

The Thinnest Rice Noodles come from Taiwan; usually used to make Banh Hoi (tiny rice sticks). See recipe on p.59.

河粉（圖 4）是米漿蒸出來的新鮮粉皮，有整大張及捲成腸狀的，也有切條的。河粉可用來炒、煮湯或包捲餡料。使用時用蒸或微波爐加熱，或在滾水內川燙以去油。另有一種新鮮細河粉（比一般新鮮河粉不油較乾），捲成一糰以真空包裝出售，專用於湯河粉（見第 67 頁）。用時在滾水內川燙，再加入高湯。如沒有新鮮細河粉可用乾河粉取代，若用乾河粉則先用水泡軟後，放入滾水川燙，再加入高湯內。

美萩粿條（圖 5）又稱美拖粿條，是用馬鈴薯粉或木薯粉製成的粉條，煮法為多量水燒開，放入粿條煮開，立即熄火蓋鍋燜 15 分鐘至呈透明狀，入口有韌性，可煮湯（見第 65 頁）或炒來吃。

瀨粉（圖 6）是用粘米粉及菱粉製成的粗粉條，與日式烏冬類似，但較有韌度，沒有粿條那麼透明。市場上有出售新鮮的瀨粉，買回來後，需置冰箱，放入湯前，可先用熱水川燙以去油，撈出後放入湯內煮開即可（見第 67 頁）。

麵（圖 7）是以麵粉製成的麵條，有粗細不同、生的、熟的、加蛋的等各種種類的麵。

以上河粉、粿條、米粉（檬）、瀨粉、麵等均可依個人喜好互相取代使用。

木薯粉（菱粉）木薯（圖 8）的澱粉有韌性，除了用來芶芡外，亦可製作鹹點當主食。

Fresh Rice Noodles (Banh Pho) (Fig.4) Made from steamed rice batter; available in large sheets, rolled like sausages, or strips. It may be used for stir-frying, wrapping fillings or in soups. To prepare, steam or heat with microwave oven, or blanch in boiling water to remove oil. Another type of fresh thin rice noodle is drier and not oily; comes in a rolled ball inside an air-tight package; used in rice noodle soups (see p.67). To use, blanch in boiling water, drain then add to stock. If fresh rice noodles are not available, may substitute with dry rice noodles. To prepare dry rice noodles, soak the noodles in water until soft, blanch in boiling water, then add to stock.

Tapioca Sticks (Fig.5) Made from water chestnut powder or tapioca starch; cooking procedures are the same as rice noodles. Place in a large amount of boiling water, turn off heat immediately, then cover for 15 minutes until they become opaque in color and are chewy. May use in soups (see p.65) or as a stir-fry.

Vietnamese Rice Noodles (Fig.6) Made from rice powder and yucca starch, these thick noodles are chewy compared to Japanese udon noodles, and are not as translucent as tapioca sticks. Asian grocery markets sell fresh Vietnamese rice noodles. They need to be refrigerated until ready to use in soups. Blanch in boiling water to remove oil, drain, and cook in soup until boiling; serve (see p.67).

Noodles (Fig.7) Are made from flour and come in a variety of thicknesses and shapes, raw, cooked, egg added, and many other different kinds.

The above kinds of noodles are interchangeable in recipes according to preferences.

Tapioca (Yucca) Starch Yucca (Fig.8) has a slight springy quality. Suitable for thickening purposes, it may be used also to make salty snacks for main dishes.

香味配料
FRAGRANT ACCOMPANIMENTS

碎花生（圖 1）炸或炒香的去衣花生壓碎，食用前放入菜餚內。

炒米碎粉（圖 2）米炒成金黃色後壓成碎粉，使用糯米較易壓，也可買現成的。

炸香紅蔥頭（圖 3）紅蔥頭切薄片放入油內，小火炒至金黃色。

油蔥 油 1 大匙燒熱，加 2 大匙蔥花炒香，可製 1 小匙油蔥。現做的顏色翠綠。

Ground Roasted Peanuts (Fig.1) Crushed deep-fried or stir-fried skinless peanuts; sprinkle on dishes before serving.

Roasted Rice Powder (Fig.2) Stir-fry rice until golden brown; crush into powder. Sweet rice is easier to crush, or purchase ready-made rice powder.

Fried Shallots (Fig.3) Slice shallots and fry in oil over low heat until golden brown.

Fried Green Onions Heat 1 T. oil, add 2 T. minced green onions, and stir-fry until fragrant. Makes 1 t. freshly fried green onions that are a vibrant green.

香草葉
FRAGRANT SPICES / HERBS

香草葉又名香花菜，每種香草葉各有獨特的香味，包括如下：

Each spice or herb has its own distinct aroma. The "fragrant spices/herbs" used in this book include the following:

九層塔 • Basil

薄荷葉 • Mint

香菜（芫荽）• Coriander(cilantro)

番芫荽 • Ngo Gai

紫蘇 • Tia To

荊芥葉 • Kinh Gioi

辣草葉 • Rau Ram

魚腥草 • Rau Dap Ca

香草葉及蔬菜
FRAGRANT SPICES/HERBS AND VEGETABLES

香草葉及蔬菜（圖 12）本書內所指的 "香草葉及蔬菜" 包含以下材料：香草葉 6 枝（九層塔、薄荷葉、香菜、番芫荽、韭菜、芹菜、紫蘇、荊芥等任選），蔬菜 2 杯（綠豆芽、生菜任選），新鮮辣椒 4 片，青檸檬 2 塊。

食用者可隨意添加上列材料於檬（米粉）或粿條的熱湯內。

Fragrant Spices/Herbs and Vegetables (Fig.12) Used in this book include: 6 sprigs of spices/herbs (choose from among basil, mint, coriander, ngo gai, chives, celery, tia to, kinh gioi, etc.), 2 c. vegetables (bean sprouts or green leaf lettuce), 4 slices fresh chili, 2 pieces lime.

Select any or some of the above listed ingredients and add to rice noodles soup or tapioca sticks soup to enhance the flavor.

酸甜蘿蔔絲及沾料
VEGETABLE ACCOMPANIMENT AND DIPPING SAUCES

傳統的越南菜，除了搭配 " '香味配料" 及 "香草葉" 還可用酸甜紅白蘿蔔絲及各式沾料與菜餚配食。因這些材料的襯托，使菜餚獨具風格。

酸甜紅白蘿蔔絲（圖 13）紅白蘿蔔共 24 兩（900 公克）切絲，加鹽 2 小匙略醃軟，沖洗握乾，加糖、醋、水各 1 杯，1 小時後即可食用。冷藏可保持兩星期。

甜酸辣魚露沾料（圖 14）糖 4 大匙及水 8 大匙燒開，待涼後與青檸檬汁（或白米醋）及魚露各 1½ 大匙，辣椒、蒜末各 1 小匙；全部攪拌混合即成，簡單易做，是一般人喜愛的沾料。加青檸檬汁的放入冰箱可保存一星期，加醋的可放一個月。

鹹魚調味沾料（圖 15）鹹魚醬、糖、青檸檬汁、醋、鳳梨汁各 2 大匙，鳳梨 2 片，辣椒、蒜末各 1 小匙；全部材料用攪拌機攪碎即成。此沾料是有鹹魚風味的特殊沾料。

海鮮醬調味沾料（圖 16）糯米粉（或玉米粉）2 大匙及高湯 1 杯攪拌燒開，加海鮮醬 2 大匙及深色醬油 ½ 小匙煮成麵糊，食時將麵糊 2 大匙加酸甜紅白蘿蔔絲 5 條及碎花生、辣椒醬各 ¼ 小匙。

Besides "fragrant accompaniments" and "fragrant spices/herbs", traditional Vietnamese cuisine also uses sweet/sour carrots and turnips and other dipping sauces to accompany dishes. These fragrant and varied additions are hallmarks of Vietnamese cuisine.

Sweet/Sour Carrots and Turnips (Fig.13) Shred 2 lbs. (900g), combine carrots and turnips, mix with 2 t. salt until slightly softened. Rinse, drain, and add 1 c. each sugar, vinegar, and water. Set 1 hour and serve. May refrigerate up to two weeks.

Sweet/Sour/Spicy Fish Sauce (Fig.14) Boil 4 T. sugar and 8 T. water; cool. Combine with 1½ T. each lime juice (or white vinegar) and fish sauce, 1 t. each chili and minced garlic. Mix thoroughly and serve. Easy to make and is a common popular dipping sauce. If made with lime juice, may keep for one week; if made with vinegar, one month.

Preserved (Mam) Fish Sauce (Fig.15) 2 T. each anchovy fish sauce, sugar, lime juice, vinegar, and pineapple juice; 2 slices pineapple; 1 t. each chili and minced garlic. Mix thoroughly in a blender and serve. The anchovies give this dipping sauce its special character.

Seasoned Hoisin Sauce (Fig. 16) Boil 2 T. sweet rice powder (or cornstarch) and 1 c. stock. Add 2 T. Hoisin sauce and ½ t. dark soy sauce; cook until pasty. When serving, use 2 T. cooked sauce, five shreds of carrots and turnips and ¼ t. each ground roasted peanuts and chili paste.

檸檬汁雞鬆
MINCED LEMON CHICKEN

⅔ lb. (300g) boneless chicken breast

☐1
- 1T. roasted rice powder (p.12)
- 1T. galangal, minced
- 3 chili peppers, minced

☐2
- ¼ c. ea. (chopped): green onions, mint leaves
- 3 T. lime juice (or white vinegar)
- 1 ½ T. fish sauce

12 lettuce or other vegetable leaves

雞胸肉… 8 兩 [300 公克]

☐1
炒米碎粉 [見 12 頁]… 1 大匙
南薑 [切碎]… 1 大匙
辣椒 [切碎]… 3 支

☐2
蔥、薄荷葉…切碎各 ¼ 杯
青檸檬汁 [或白醋]… 3 大匙
魚露… 1½ 大匙
生菜 [或其他蔬菜]… 12 片

1 雞肉切成薄片，用油煎至二面呈金黃色 [或烤熟]，肉不宜煎太熟，以免太乾。
2 煎好的雞肉切碎，拌入 ☐1 及 ☐2 料，用生菜包裹。與糯米飯配食是傳統吃法。
■ 可依喜好選用不同的肉類，如魚、牛、豬等。傳統做法是在雞肉內加雞肫，牛肉則加切絲牛百葉。

1 Cut chicken breast into thin slices, and pan-fry (or bake) until golden brown. Do not over-cook or meat will be too dry.
2 Mince the cooked chicken; mix in ☐1 and ☐2 then serve wrapped in lettuce. Traditionally served with steamed sweet rice.
■ Instead of chicken, may also substitute fish, beef, or pork. The traditional recipe calls for chicken gizzards in addition to breast meat; when using beef, add tripe shreds.

香草葉燒雞
FRAGRANT HERB CHICKEN

1 ⅛ lbs. (600g) chicken, cut in pieces

☐1
- 1 T. minced garlic
- 1 T. minced lemon grass (or ginger)

☐2
- 1 T. ea.: oyster sauce, soy sauce, cooking wine, water
- 1 t. ea.: sugar, chili paste

1 c. fresh basil leaves (or tia to)

帶骨雞 [剁塊]… 1 斤 [600 公克]

☐1
蒜末… 1 大匙
香茅 [或薑]…切碎 1 大匙

☐2
蠔油、醬油、酒、水…各 1 大匙
糖、辣椒醬…各 1 小匙
九層塔葉 [或紫蘇]… 1 杯

1 油 2 大匙燒熱，放入 ☐1 料炒香，隨入雞塊炒至八分熟，再入 ☐2 料翻炒後，蓋上鍋蓋，煮至汁收乾，加入九層塔即成。
■ "香草葉燒雞"原本使用田雞為材料，本食譜採用大眾化的雞肉，亦不失其美味；除此之外，魷魚、蜆、豬肉均可應用。

1 Heat 2 T. oil, add ☐1 and stir-fry until fragrant. Add chicken pieces and cook until 80% done. Add ☐2, mix and stir-fry; cover and cook until liquid evaporates. Add basil leaves.
■ "Fragrant Herb Chicken" originally used frogs. While this cookbook lists chicken, the more commonly used ingredient, the flavor is not compromised. May also use squid, clams, or pork.

香草葉燒雞 · *FRAGRANT HERB CHICKEN*
椰汁雞腿 · *COCONUT CHICKEN DRUM STICKS*

椰汁雞腿
COCONUT CHICKEN DRUM STICKS

雞腿 6 支… 1 斤 [600 公克]

☐1
紅蔥頭、蔥…搗碎共 4 大匙
法國香葉… 4 片

☐2
魚露… 2 大匙
胡椒… ¼ 小匙
椰汁… 2 杯，辣椒絲… ½ 大匙

1 雞腿洗淨，瀝乾水份，拌入 ☐1 及 ☐2 料，醃 1 小時。
2 油 1 大匙燒熱，將雞腿表面煎黃，隨入椰汁及雞腿醃汁煮開，改中火煮 20 分鐘，至汁略收乾時放入辣椒絲即可起鍋，與飯配食。

☐1
- 6 chicken legs, 1 ⅛ lbs. (600g)
- 4 T. total (mashed): shallots, green onions
- 4 bay leaf slices

☐2
- 2 T. fish sauce
- ¼ t. pepper
- 2 c. coconut juice
- ½ T. shredded chili pepper

1 Wash chicken legs, drain. Mix in ☐1 and ☐2, marinate 1 hour.
2 Heat 1 T. oil, pan-fry chicken legs until surface is golden. Add coconut juice and marinade sauce; cook until boiling. Reduce to medium heat and cook 20 minutes, until liquid evaporates somewhat, then add shredded chili pepper. Serve with steamed rice.

滷水鴨
STEWED WATER FOWL

鴨 1 隻 ……………4 斤 [2400 公克]
鹽………3 大匙，糖………4 大匙

1
老抽 [或醬油]、魚露……各 3 大匙
水 …………………………2 杯

2
八角 [圖 1] …………………4 朵
茴香子 [圖 2] ………………¼ 杯
南薑 …………………………8 片
蒜頭 [略拍] ………………10 瓣

3
米醋 …………………………1½ 大匙
魚露 …………………………1 小匙
蒜末、辣椒末、香菜末………隨意

1 鴨去除內臟、肥油，洗淨後用鹽塗抹鴨身內外。置 4 小時後，用清水大略沖洗備用。

2 將糖放入乾鍋內，以小火炒呈咖啡色的糖漿，隨入 **1** 料燒滾，放入鴨及內臟，邊淋汁邊翻面，煮至鴨表面上色，再加水滿過鴨身 7 分處，加 **2** 料煮開，蓋鍋以中火煮約 50 分鐘至熟撈出 [中間需翻面，以免燒焦]，待涼剁塊，沾 **3** 料或其他沾料食用。

■ 使用老抽及糖漿的用意僅是為了色澤，老抽因廠牌不同，顏色深淺各異。也可將老抽及醬油混合使用。燒煮後的剩餘滷汁，可斟酌加水用來滷豬蹄膀、豬舌、牛腱、及豆腐乾等。

1 duck, 5 ⅓ lbs. (2400g)
3 T. salt
4 T. sugar

1
3 T. dark soy sauce
** (or soy sauce)**
3 T. fish sauce
2 c. water

2
4 star anises (Fig. 1)
¼ c. fennel seeds (Fig. 2)
8 galangal slices
10 garlic cloves, slightly
** mashed**

3
1 ½ T. rice vinegar
1 t. fish sauce
minced garlic, chili pepper and
** coriander as desired**

1 Remove innards and fat from duck, wash, then rub salt inside and out. Set 4 hours, rinse with water, then set aside.

2 With low heat, stir-fry sugar in pan until it becomes brown syrup. Add **1**, bring to boil. Add duck and innards, baste duck with juice while cooking, until duck turns color. Cover 70% of duck with water, add **2** and bring to boil. Cover and cook in medium heat 50 minutes (must turn while cooking to prevent burning); remove and cool. Cut into pieces and serve with **3** or other sauces.

■ Dark soy sauce and sugar are used for their dark color. Because different companies make dark soy sauce, its shades of darkness vary greatly. May also mix dark soy sauce with regular soy sauce. The remaining marinade sauce may be diluted with water to stew pork hock, pork tongue, beef shank, and pressed bean curd.

咖哩鴨
CURRY DUCK

鴨 ½ 隻 ················1 斤 [600 公克]

① 魚露 ····3 大匙，咖哩粉 ····1½ 大匙

　印度咖哩籽 ······················1 小匙

② 蒜末 ·····························1 大匙
　香茅 [切段] ····················2 支
　洋蔥 [切塊] ····················1½ 杯

③ 法國香葉 [或泰國檸檬葉] ······5 片
　水 ······························4 杯
　糖 ······························2 小匙
　鹽 ······························¼ 小匙

④ 鳳梨 [切塊] ··········4 兩 [150 公克]
　茄子 [切塊煮熟] ·····4 兩 [150 公克]

　椰奶 [或鮮奶] ·····················½ 杯

⑤ 青檸檬汁 ·····················½ 大匙
　辣椒 [切片] ····················1 支

1 鴨剁塊，用 ① 料醃 20 分鐘。

2 油 2 大匙燒熱，用小火將咖哩籽炒香，油的顏色呈紅色，咖哩籽變黑即撈出不要 [此過程可增加菜餚的顏色]。

3 隨即炒香 ② 料，再入鴨及醃汁炒至鴨表面變色，續加 ③ 料，煮開除泡沫，蓋鍋以小火煮 30 分鐘至熟軟，加 ④ 料燒開後改小火，加入椰奶拌勻煮開。食用時再加 ⑤ 料，可與麵包或飯搭配。

■ 如果分二次吃，留下的半份加熱時再加椰奶，如此較能儲存。

■ 在越南用咖哩做的菜餚很普遍，可用雞、牛、豬、或魚取代鴨，④ 料可改用紅蘿蔔、馬鈴薯、小洋蔥或蕃薯等。市面上有現成的紅色或綠色咖哩醬 [圖 1]，種類很多，口味也不一樣。若用現成咖哩醬則可免用 ① 及 ② 料。

■ 按不同主食的搭配，咖哩湯汁燒煮的濃度則不同。配麵包的咖哩湯汁較濃，配其他的主食例如"咖哩鴨檬"則較稀。

咖哩鴨檬 碗內備檬，加入略煮稀的"咖哩鴨"後再加魚露調味即成。

½ duck, 1 ⅓ lbs. (600g)

① **3 T. fish sauce**
1 ½ T. curry powder

1 t. annatto seeds

② **1 T. minced garlic**
2 lemon grass, sectioned
1 ½ c. onion pieces

③ **5 bay leaf slices**
(or kaffir leaves)
4 c. water
2 t. sugar
¼ t. salt

④ **⅓ lb. (150g) pineapple pieces**
⅓ lb. (150g) cooked eggplant
pieces

½ c. coconut milk (or milk)

⑤ **½ T. lime juice**
1 chili pepper, sliced

1 Cut duck into pieces, marinate with ① for 20 minutes.

2 Heat 2 T. oil, stir-fry annatto seeds in low heat until fragrant. The oil takes on a reddish color (this step adds color to this dish); remove the darkened annatto seeds.

3 Stir-fry ②, add duck and marinade; stir-fry until duck changes color. Add ③ and bring to boil; remove suds. Cover and simmer in low heat 30 minutes until duck softens. Add ④ and bring to boil, reduce heat to low, mix in coconut milk and bring to boil. Add ⑤ when serving; may serve with bread or steamed rice.

■ If divided into two meals, add coconut milk to the second portion when reheating to better preserve freshness.

■ In Vietnam, curry is a commonly used ingredient. Chicken, beef, pork, or fish, may be used for duck. Carrots, potatoes, small onions, or sweet potatoes may be used for ④. Markets sell ready-made red or green curry sauce (Fig.1), in many varieties and flavors. If using ready-made curry sauce, omit ① and ②.

■ The thickness of the curry duck broth varies depending on accompanying staples. When served with bread, a thicker broth is best while "curry duck with rice noodles" requires a thinner broth.

Curry Duck With Rice Noodles Put rice noodles in bowl, top with curry duck cooked in thinner broth, then add fish sauce to taste.

香煎牛肉
FRAGRANT PAN-FRIED BEEF

瘦牛肉[眼肉][切片]·8 兩[300 公克]

① 蠔油、醬油 .... 各 1 大匙

油 .... 1 大匙
油蔥 [見 12 頁] .... 1 小匙
芝麻 [炒香] [或碎花生] .... 1 小匙

⅔ lb. (300g) eye of round beef,
sliced

① 1 T. oyster sauce
1 T. soy sauce

1 T. oil
1 t. fried green onion (p. 12)
1 t. roasted sesame or ground
roasted peanuts

1 牛肉拌入 ① 料醃 20 分鐘，煎前再拌入油。

2 鍋燒熱，在鍋面抹一層油，大火二面煎至金黃色即鏟入盤內，上撒油蔥及芝麻；可用米紙、生菜包捲，沾"甜酸辣魚露沾料"[見 13 頁]食用，也可配飯。

■ 其他食用法見 59 頁 "檳海" 及 "檬"。

1 Mix ① into beef, marinate 20 minutes. Mix with oil before pan-frying.

2 Heat pan, coat pan with oil, fry using high heat until both sides are golden brown. Remove and sprinkle with fried green onions and sesame. May serve with steamed rice, or wrap with rice paper or lettuce, then dip in "sweet/sour/spicy fish sauce" (p.13).

■ See p.59 for serving alternatives using tiny rice sticks and rice noodles.

牛肉蝦醋窩
BEEF AND TART SHRIMP WRAP

① 牛肉片 .... 6 兩 [225 公克]
蝦 [去殼] .... 12 隻

② 醋 .... ½ 杯，水 .... 1 杯
炸香紅蔥頭 [見 12 頁] ...... ½ 小匙
碎花生 [見 12 頁] .... ¼ 小匙

③ 香草葉 [見 12 頁] .... 24 片
生菜 .... 6 片

米紙 [直徑 20 公分] .... 12 張
甜酸辣魚露沾料或鹹魚調味沾料
[見 13 頁] .... 適量

① ½ lb. (225g) beef slices
12 shelled shrimp

② ½ c. vinegar, 1 c. water
½ t. fried shallots (p. 12)
¼ t. ground roasted peanuts
(p. 12)

③ 24 slices of fragrant
spices/herbs (p. 12)
6 lettuce leaves

12 sheets of rice paper
(diameter 8", 20cm)
sweet/sour/spicy fish sauce or
preserved (mam) fish sauce
(p. 13) as desired

1 將 ①、③ 料及泡軟米紙[見 10 頁]備於盤內。

2 將 ② 料燒開，隨意取 ① 料[亦可隨喜好加魷魚、干貝等]，放入湯內煮熟，隨即撈出置於米紙內與適量 ③ 料包捲後，沾上沾料食用。

■ 此種菜餚在桌上邊煮邊食，樂趣無比。越南有名的 "牛肉七味"，包括 "牛肉蝦醋窩"、 "香煎牛肉" 及其他五種牛肉菜餚。

1 Prepare ① and ③, soften rice paper in water (p.10). Set aside on plates.

2 Boil ②, cook desired amounts of ① (may also use squid, scallops, and other favorites). Remove when cooked and wrap in rice paper, using desired amounts of ③, serve with dipping sauce.

■ The fun in this dish is in its serve-while-cooking approach. Vietnam's famous "Seven-Flavored Beef" includes "Beef and Tart Shrimp Wrap", "Fragrant Pan-Fried Beef", and five other beef delicacies.

茄汁牛肉
BEEF IN TOMATO SAUCE

牛肉 [切塊]............1 斤 [600 公克]
魚露......3 大匙，番茄醬泥......6 大匙

① 蒜末、辣椒末............共 2 大匙
洋蔥塊......1½ 杯，南薑......14 片

② 水............6 杯，鹽......¼ 小匙
泰國檸檬葉 [或法國香葉]............4 片

③ 紅、白蘿蔔......切塊共 8 兩 [300 公克]

青檸檬汁............½ 大匙

1 牛肉川燙瀝乾，用魚露醃 20 分鐘。

2 油 2 大匙依序炒香 ① 料，隨入牛肉及醃汁略炒至肉表面變色，加番茄醬泥略炒，續加 ② 料煮開，去除泡沫，蓋鍋以小火煮 1½ 小時再加 ③ 料，煮 30 分鐘至 ③ 料及肉熟軟，熄火，加入青檸檬汁。可與麵包或飯配食。

茄汁牛肉粉 碗內備河粉及豆芽菜，加略煮稀的"茄汁牛肉"，再加魚露調味即成。

1 Blanch beef, drain, marinate 20 minutes in fish sauce.

2 Heat 2 T. oil and stir-fry in order ①, followed by beef and marinade until meat changes color. Add tomato paste, lightly stir-fry, followed by ②; bring to boil. Remove suds, cover and cook 1½ hours in low heat. Add ③, cook 30 minutes until ③ and meat soften. Turn off heat and add lime juice. Serve with bread or steamed rice.

Beef in Tomato Sauce on Noodles Put fresh rice noodles and bean sprouts in bowl, and add thinned "Beef in Tomato Sauce". Top with fish sauce and serve.

1 ⅛ lbs. (600g) beef, cut in pieces
3 T. fish sauce, 6 T. tomato paste

① 2 T. total (minced): garlic, chili pepper
1 ½ c. onion pieces
14 galangal slices

② 6 c. water, ¼ t. salt
4 kaffir leaves (or bay leaves)

③ ⅔ lb. (300g) total (cut in pieces): carrots and turnips

½ T. lime juice

檸檬牛肉
LEMON BEEF

瘦牛肉 [切片]............8 兩 [300 公克]

① 油............1 小匙，蛋白............1 個
玉米粉............1 大匙
蒜末............1 大匙

② 魚露............1½ 大匙
玉米粉、水............各 2 小匙

③ 胡椒......¼ 小匙，青檸檬汁 ....1 大匙

④ 辣椒、香菜......切小段共 2 大匙

1 牛肉拌入 ① 料醃 20 分鐘。

2 油 2 大匙燒熱，炒香蒜末，隨入牛肉炒至變色，再加拌勻的 ② 料炒拌均勻，熄火，上撒 ③、④ 料。此道菜做法簡單且開胃。

⅔ lb. (300g) lean beef slices

① 1 t. oil, 1 egg white
1 T. cornstarch
1 T. minced garlic

② 1 ½ T. fish sauce
2 t. ea.: cornstarch, water

③ ¼ t. pepper
1 T. lime juice

④ 2 T. total (sectioned): chili pepper, coriander

1 Mix ① with beef and marinate 20 minutes.

2 Heat 2 T. oil, stir-fry minced garlic until fragrant, followed by beef. Cook until meat changes color, add well-mixed ②, stir-fry and mix thoroughly. Turn off heat, sprinkle ③ and ④. This dish is easy to prepare and appetizing.

檸檬牛肉 · *LEMON BEEF*
沙茶牛肉 · *SA-TSA BEEF*

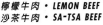

沙茶牛肉
SA-TSA BEEF

牛肉 [切片]............8 兩 [300 公克]
① 同"檸檬牛肉" ① 料
② 沙茶醬............¼ 杯，水............1 杯

③ 鮮奶............¼ 杯
魚露............1 大匙
辣椒絲............1 小匙

1 牛肉拌入 ① 料。

2 將 ② 料拌勻後燒滾，加入 ③ 料再燒開，隨將醃好的肉每次少量放入湯汁內燙熟，取出置於盤內，全部燙熟，剩餘的湯汁淋在牛肉上，可配番茄、黃瓜。與飯食用。

沙茶粿條 美萩粿條放入碗底，上淋"沙茶牛肉"再配番茄及黃瓜即成。

⅔ lb. (300g) beef slices
① same as ① of "Lemon Beef"
② ¼ c. barbecue (sa-tsa) sauce
1 c. water

③ ¼ c. milk
1 T. fish sauce
1 t. shredded chili pepper

1 Mix beef with ①.

2 Mix well ② then bring to boil, add ③ and boil again. Take small amounts of marinated beef and cook in boiling sauce; remove each portion when cooked and place on plate. After cooking all portions, baste beef with remaining sauce. Serve with steamed rice, tomatoes and cucumber.

Sa-tsa Tapioca Sticks Put tapioca sticks in bowl, top with sa-tsa beef, tomatoes and cucumber; serve.

豬肉燜高麗菜
SIMMERED PORK AND CABBAGE

豬肉 [夾心肉] 4 片 6 兩 [225 公克]
醬油 ·······1⅓ 大匙
高麗菜或大白菜··12 兩 [450 公克]

① 香菇 [泡軟] ·······4 朵
胡椒 ·······¼ 小匙
水 ·······1⅓ 杯

4 pork pieces*, ½ lb. (225g)
1 ⅛ T. soy sauce
1 lb. (450g) cabbage or napa
cabbage

① **4 presoftened Chinese black**
mushrooms
¼ t. pepper
1 ⅛ c. water

1 豬肉用醬油醃 20 分鐘，高麗菜切 5 大塊備用。

2 油 2 大匙燒熱，將高麗菜兩面煎呈金黃色。

3 油 1 大匙燒熱，將肉二面煎黃，隨入醃肉汁、高麗菜及 ① 料，煮開後蓋鍋以小火燜煮，煮到中途時把下面的肉置於高麗菜上，以便均勻燒煮各料，煮 20 分鐘至湯汁略收乾。與飯配食。

■ 高麗菜切大塊，燒煮出來的效果佳。菜內略含湯汁非常可口，有葷有素，是一道理想的簡餐。

1 Marinate pork in soy sauce for 20 minutes. Cut cabbage into large pieces and set aside.

2 Heat 2 T. oil, pan-fry cabbage until golden brown.

3 Heat 1 T. oil, pan-fry pork until both sides are golden brown, add marinade, cabbage and ①. Bring to boil, cover, and simmer in low heat. To ensure even cooking of all ingredients, place meat on top of the cabbage at mid-point in cooking. Cook 20 minutes until broth evaporates somewhat. Serve with steamed rice.

★ Use pork containing fat for best flavor.

■ Large pieces of cabbage are ideal to bring out the flavor of the broth. This simple dish is ideal since it contains both meat and vegetables.

煎豬扒
PAN-FRIED PORK CHOPS

豬大排肉 *4 片····12 兩 [450 公克]

① 醬油 ·······2 大匙
魚露、玉米粉 ·······各 1 大匙
糖 ·······2 小匙
辣椒粉 ·······½ 小匙

② 蒜頭 [略拍] ·······3 瓣
紅蔥頭 [切薄片] ·······4 顆
香菜莖 [略切] ·······1 大匙

4 pork chops*, 1 lb. (450g)

① **2 T. soy sauce**
1 T. fish sauce
2 t. sugar
1 T. cornstarch
½ t. chili powder

② **3 garlic cloves, slightly mashed**
4 shallots, sliced
1 T. coriander stem pieces,
sectioned

1 將 ② 料搗碎，加入 ① 料成醃料。

2 用刀背或搥肉器把豬大排肉搥鬆，調入醃料醃 1 小時，中間翻拌 2 或 3 次 [若不急用，① 料內多加蘇打粉 ⅛ 小匙，醃隔夜則可免搥肉的手續]。

3 油 3 大匙燒熱，大火把表面煎呈金黃色至肉熟，共需 5 分鐘。

★ 豬大排肉周圍的筋須用刀切小缺口，以免豬排加熱時捲曲。也可用雞胸肉取代豬排。

1 Mash ② and add ① to make marinade.

2 Tenderize pork chops with the back of a cleaver blade or a wooden meat tenderizer. Marinate with above marinade for 1 hour, stirring 2 - 3 times during the hour (if not in a hurry, add ⅛ t. baking soda to ①, marinate overnight to omit tenderizing meat by hand).

3 Heat 3 T. oil, pan-fry in high heat until meat is cooked and golden brown, about 5 minutes.

★ Make small incisions into tendon surrounding pork chop to avoid curling when pan-frying. May substitute chicken breast for pork chops.

豆腐餅
TOFU CASSEROLE

豆腐 1 盒 ·············12 兩 [450 公克]

① 蠔油······2 大匙, 胡椒 ······¼ 小匙
麻油······1 小匙, 玉米粉····1 大匙

② 火腿 [切小片] ···················⅓ 杯
冬粉泡軟 [切小段]···············⅓ 杯
香菇泡軟 [切小片]···············⅓ 杯
蔥花···························2 大匙

起士····························10 片
烤盤 [15x15 公分]··············1 個

1 烤盤內塗一層油備用。

2 將豆腐擠乾水份,搗成泥狀,先拌入 ① 料再加 ② 料攪拌,裝入烤盤內略壓平,上面均勻的鋪一層起士後,隨意加些裝飾在上面。烤盤內豆腐勿裝太滿,以免烤時起士溢出。

3 烤箱預熱 350°F [180°C],烤 35 分鐘至表面呈金黃色;若用蒸的,水燒開,將豆腐餅大火蒸 20 分鐘即可。

■ 此道菜可用起士絲取代起士片,均勻地撒在豆腐上。豆腐不適合用嫩豆腐;豆腐餅待冷切片,可當前菜。

one package of tofu, 1 lb. (450g)

① **2 T. oyster sauce, ¼ t. pepper**
1 t. sesame oil, 1 T. cornstarch

② **⅓ c. ham, cut in small pieces**
**⅓ c. pre-softened bean threads,
cut in small sections**
**⅓ c. pre-softened Chinese
black mushrooms, cut in
small pieces**
2 T. chopped green onions

**10 cheese slices
baking pan, (6"x6", 15x15cm)**

1 Lightly grease baking pan with oil.

2 Squeeze water from tofu, mash, mix with ①. Add ② then mix thoroughly. Fill pan with mixture and gently level; layer evenly with cheese, and top with any decorations. Do not fill pan with too much tofu or the cheese will spill during baking.

3 Heat oven to 350°F(180°C), bake 35 minutes until golden brown. If steaming is desired, steam tofu over boiling water at high heat for 20 minutes.

■ May substitute shredded cheese for sliced cheese, sprinkle evenly over tofu. Soft tofu is not ideal for this dish. When cooled, cut tofu casserole into slices and serve as an appetizer.

肉烤蛋
BAKED PORK AND EGGS

雞蛋 *····························4 個

① 絞肉 ·················6 兩 [225 公克]
鹹魚肉 * [切碎] ·················¼ 杯
木耳泡軟 [切碎]·················¼ 杯
蒜末····························1 小匙
辣椒 [切碎]·····················½ 小匙

② 油······1 小匙, 玉米粉······2 小匙

烤盤 [15x15 公分]··············1 個

1 將 ① 料及 ② 料略拌後先放入一個蛋白,仔細攪拌均勻後再加第二個,直到全部加完,攪拌至有黏性成為肉漿。蛋黃打散留用。

2 烤盤內塗油放入肉漿,蓋上鋁鉑紙,上戳 4 個小洞,烤箱預熱 350°F [180°C] 烤 40 分鐘。拿掉鋁鉑紙淋入蛋黃後,隨意加些裝飾在上面,再烤 10 分鐘即可。也可用蒸的;與飯配食。

★ 越南人喜歡用鴨蛋代替雞蛋,烤出來的顏色比較金黃。若使用乾的鹹魚肉,先略炒過可增香味;也可用炒過的碎蝦米或醃花瓜取代鹹魚肉,使用醃花瓜則多加鹽 ½ 小匙。

4 eggs*

① **½ lb. (225g) ground pork**
**¼ c. preserved (mam) fish*,
minced**
**¼ c. presoftened dried wood
ears, minced**
1 t. minced garlic
½ t. minced chili pepper

② **1 t. oil**
2 t. cornstarch

baking pan (6"x6", 15x15cm)

1 Mix ① and ②, add one egg white, then mix thoroughly. Add remaining egg whites, one at a time, and mix thoroughly until mixture becomes a sticky meat paste. Beat egg yolks and set aside.

2 Pre-heat oven to 350°F(180°C). Grease pan with oil, fill with meat paste, and cover with foil. Poke four holes into foil. Bake 40 minutes. Remove foil and drizzle with egg yolk, add any desired decorations, then bake an additional 10 minutes. May also steam; serve with steamed rice.

★ The Vietnamese prefer duck eggs because the resulting gold color is more intense. If using dried, preserved fish, stir-fry first to enhance flavor; may also use stir-fried and minced dried shrimp or pickled cucumber instead of preserved fish. If using pickled cucumber, add ½ t. salt.

扎肉 (越南火腿)
PORK MEAT LOAF (VIETNAMESE HAM)

4 人份 · Serves 4

①	雞胸肉	8 兩 [300 公克]
	瘦豬肉	4 兩 [150 公克]
②	鹽	¼ 小匙
	發粉 [或蘇打粉]	1 小匙
	糖	1 大匙
	玉米粉	1 大匙
	蒜末	1 大匙
	魚露	1½ 大匙
	水	3½ 大匙

香蕉葉 [30 公分四方] .... 1 張
保鮮膜 [30 公分四方] .... 1 張
鋁鉑紙 [30 公分四方] .... 1 張
棉繩 [75 公分] .... 2 條

1 將 ① 料切小薄片，放入攪肉機內攪爛，加入 ② 料，再把肉攪爛成肉泥。

2 香蕉葉攤開 [如不夠大，可數塊拼起來用]，放入肉泥包好，再用保鮮膜包固定成圓柱形，外面再以鋁鉑紙包密，拿棉繩綁好，置於冰箱 8 小時。

3 水開，將扎肉大火蒸 40 分鐘。涼後置冰箱，可保存一星期，隨時取用。

■ "扎肉" 一般以雞及豬二種肉混合，顏色較白。也可用牛肉加蒔蘿葉或豬皮做成各種風味特殊的扎肉。肉泥可用來做肉丸子，放入湯內或煎或做其他用途。

■ 香蕉葉在中國超市冷凍部門可買到，用時洗淨拭乾。

扎肉沙垃　"扎肉" 4 兩 [150 公克]，番茄、黃瓜、紅蘿蔔，或其他蔬菜 (切片或切絲) 共 12 兩 [450 公克]，淋上 "甜酸辣魚露沾料" [見 13 頁]，即成熱帶風味沙拉。

① ⅔ lb. (300g) boneless chicken breast
⅓ lb. (150g) lean pork

② ¼ t. salt
1 t. baking powder (or baking soda)
1 T. ea.: sugar, cornstarch, minced garlic
1 ½ T. fish sauce
3 ½ T. water

1 banana leaf (12"x12", 30x30cm)
1 sheet of plastic wrap (12"x12", 30x30cm)
1 sheet of aluminum foil (12"x12", 30x30cm)
2 cotton threads (30", 75cm)

1 Cut ① into small thin slices, grind in meat grinder. Add ②, then grind well into paste.

2 Spread open banana leaf (if not large enough, piece several together), wrap meat paste with leaf and secure with plastic wrap to make a cylinder. Wrap cylinder tightly with foil and tie with cotton threads. Refrigerate 8 hours.

3 Boil water, steam ham cylinder over high heat 40 minutes. Cool, then refrigerate; keeps for one week. Use as desired.

■ "Pork meat loaf" is commonly made of a mixture of pork and chicken, which yields a lighter color. May also use beef with dill or pork skin to create a different variety of meat loaf. Meat paste made in procedure 1 may also be used to make meatballs for use in soups, pan-frying, or other dishes.

■ Banana leaves are available in a Chinese markets' refrigerated section. Wash then dry before use.

Pork Meat Loaf Salad　Shred or slice ⅓ lb. (150g) "Vietnamese ham", and 1 lb. (450g) total of tomatoes, cucumbers, carrots, or other vegetables, drizzle "sweet/sour/spicy fish sauce" (p.13) and serve this tropical flavored salad.

扎肉腸粉
PORK MEAT LOAF RICE ROLLS

2 人份 · Serves 2

腸粉 *[切段]	12 兩 [450 公克]
豆芽菜	2 杯
黃瓜 [切絲]	½ 杯
九層塔 [切絲]	10 片
番茄	4 片
炸香紅蔥頭 [見 12 頁]	2 小匙
扎肉	8 片
豬皮肉絲 [見 79 頁]	⅔ 杯
甜酸辣魚露沾料 [見 13 頁]	隨意

1 先將腸粉、豆芽菜置盤內。用微波爐加熱，隨後加上扎肉及豬皮肉絲、黃瓜、九層塔、番茄、炸香紅蔥頭，淋上 "甜酸辣魚露沾料" 拌食。

★ 米漿蒸出來的新鮮粉皮 [河粉]，捲成筒狀即為 "腸粉"，市面上有現成的出售；由冰箱內取出時，加少許水，用微波爐加熱，微溫時食用較有彈性。

1 lb. (450g) fresh rice rolls*, sectioned
2 c. bean sprouts
½ c. shredded cucumber
10 fresh basil leaves, shredded
4 tomato slices
2 t. fried shallots (p. 12)
8 slices of pork meat loaf
⅔ c. shredded pork skin (p. 79)
sweet/sour/spicy fish sauce (p. 13) as desired

1 Place rice rolls and bean sprouts on plates. Warm with microwave oven, add pork meat loaf, shredded pork skin, cucumber, fresh basil, tomato, and fried shallots. Drizzle "sweet/sour/spicy fish sauce".

★ Steamed rice batter becomes fresh rice sheets, when rolled into flutes, they become "rice rolls". Available fresh in markets. When using, remove from refrigerator, add a little bit of water, and microwave to lukewarm temperature to yield elasticity.

SKEWERED CHARBROILED MEATBALLS

豬絞肉 ················· 12 兩 [450 公克]

① 糖 ···································· 1 大匙
　 鹽 ··································· ¼ 小匙
　 發粉 [或鬆肉粉] ················· 1 小匙
　 玉米粉、水、蒜末 ········ 各 2 小匙
　 洋蔥 [切碎] ······················ 2 大匙

竹籤 [20 公分] ······················ 9 支
海鮮醬調味沾料或其他沾料
[見 13 頁] ···························· 適量

1 lb. (450g) ground pork

① **1 T. sugar**
¼ t. salt
1 t. baking powder
(or tenderizing powder)
2 t. cornstarch
2 t. water
2 t. minced garlic
2 T. minced onion

9 skewers, 8" (20cm) long
seasoned hoisin sauce or
other sauces (p. 13) as
desired

1

1 將絞肉拌入 ① 料，仔細攪拌至有黏性，冷藏 8 小時，取出做 36 個丸子。可將多量絞肉 1 次調好，分袋放入冰凍，隨時取用非常方便。

2 烤箱預熱 500°F [260°C]，肉丸子擺於烤架上，烤架置烤盤內，烤半熟時，用竹籤串好，再烤至兩面呈焦黃狀，前後需 40 分鐘。肉丸串可當前菜，吃時沾 "海鮮醬調味沾料"，並與切片楊桃或酸味菜 [圖 1] 配食，是肉丸串吃法的一大特色。

■ 其他食法可參考 59 頁的 "檳海" 及 "檬" 或與飯搭配。傳統做法是用炭火烤。竹籤兩頭用鋁鉑紙稍蓋以免烤焦。

1 Mix ① with ground pork until mixture becomes sticky, refrigerate 8 hours. Remove from refrigerator, make 36 meatballs. May prepare a large quantity of ground meat mixture, divide into portions, store in freezer bags and freeze for convenient future use.

2 Heat oven to 500°F(260°C), place meatballs on a rack, then put the rack in a baking pan, bake until meatballs are halfway done. Skewer then continue baking until both sides appear brown and slightly singed. Total baking time is 40 minutes. Skewered meatballs may be served as an appetizer; dip in "seasoned hoisin sauce" and accompany with sliced star fruit or French sorrel (Fig.1). This serving method is what makes Skewered Charbroiled Meatballs unique.

■ See p.59 for serving alternatives such as rice noodles and tiny rice sticks, or serve with steamed rice. Barbecuing over charcoal is the traditional way to cook this dish. Wrap both ends of skewers with foil to prevent singeing.

SKEWERED CHARBROILED PORK

豬肉 [夾心肉] ········ 8 兩 [300 公克]

① 蒜、香茅 ············· 切碎共 1 大匙
　 蠔油 ································· 1 大匙
　 醬油 ································· 1 大匙
　 糖 ···································· 1 小匙
　 油 ···································· 1 小匙
　 辣椒粉 ······························ ½ 小匙

竹籤 [20 公分] ······················ 8 支

⅔ lb. (300g) pork*

① **1 T. total (minced): garlic,**
lemon grass
1 T. oyster sauce
1 T. soy sauce
1 t. ea.: sugar, oil
½ t. chili powder

8 skewers, 8" (20cm) long

1 豬肉切 2 公分寬、 15 公分長薄片，調入 ① 料醃 1 小時。

2 肉片用竹籤串起，共串 8 支。

3 烤箱預熱 500°F [260°C]，將肉串放在烤架上，烤架置烤盤內，放入烤 20 分鐘至二面呈焦黃狀即可。肉串可當前菜。

■ 其他食法可參考 59 頁的 "檳海" 及 "檬" 或與飯搭配。傳統做法是用炭火烤。竹籤兩頭用鋁鉑紙稍蓋以免烤焦。

1 Cut pork into ¾ inch (2cm) wide and 6 inch (15cm) long thin slices, mix with ① and marinate 1 hour.

2 Skewer meat on 8 skewers.

3 Heat oven to 500°F(260°C), place skewered meat on a rack, then put the rack in a baking pan, bake 20 minutes until both sides are brown and slightly singed. May serve as an appetizer.

＊ Use pork containing fat for best flavor

■ See p.59 for serving alternatives such as rice noodles and tiny rice sticks, or serve with steamed rice. Barbecuing over charcoal is the traditional way to cook this dish. Wrap both ends of skewers with foil to prevent singeing.

越式三明治
VIETNAMESE SANDWICH

法式麵包 [25 公分長] ············2 條

1 美奶滋、肝醬 ············各 2 小匙
奶油 ·······················1 小匙

2 扎肉 [見 29 頁]、扎蹄肉、
美式火腿、黃瓜、辣椒···各 4 片
香菜 ·······················4 支
酸甜紅白蘿蔔絲 [見 13 頁]·2 大匙

3 醬油···1 小匙,胡椒 ·········少許

1 麵包放入烤箱烤 3 分鐘至表皮脆取出,由中間切開成夾狀。

2 打開麵包,中間先均勻塗上 ① 料,再夾入 ② 料及 ③ 料,趁麵包還脆時食用。

■ 三明治若當野餐不馬上吃,則食用前再加入 "酸甜紅白蘿蔔絲",以免變質。

■ 可隨喜好夾入不同的肉類,如烤肉、肉絲豬皮[見 79 頁]、燒賣[見 33 頁]、罐頭沙丁魚等。

2 loaves of French bread,
10" (25cm)

1 **2 t. ea.: mayonnaise,**
pate (liverwurst)
1 t. butter

2 **4 slices ea.: pork meat loaf**
(p. 29) , cured pork roll
sausage, ham, cucumber,
chili pepper
4 coriander branches
2 T. sweet/sour carrots and
turnips (p. 13)

3 **1 t. soy sauce**
pepper as desired

1 Warm bread in oven 3 minutes, remove when crust is crispy. Slice open to contain filling.

2 Spread ① on both sides of bread, insert ② and then ③. Serve while bread is warm.

■ If not serving sandwiches right away, such as preparing for picnic or lunch, "sweet/sour carrots and turnips" should be set aside and added to the sandwich before serving to prevent spoiling.

■ As desired, use different types of meat, such as barbecued meat or shredded pork skin (p.79), shau mai (p.33), or canned sardines.

越式燒賣
VIETNAMESE SHAU MAI

1 豬絞肉 ·············½ 斤 [300 公克]
蝦仁 [切丁] ·······4 兩 [150 公克]

2 蛋白···1 個,魚露、水···各 2 大匙
糖、油、麻油 ·········各 ¾ 小匙
胡椒 ······¼ 小匙,玉米粉···1 大匙

3 蒜末···1 小匙,蔥花···1 大匙

4 番茄丁、水 ·············各 ½ 杯
魚露、番茄醬 ·········各 1 大匙
糖 ·······1 小匙,玉米粉···2 小匙

麵包 ·······················4 個

1 將 ① 料加入 ② 料,仔細用力攪拌至有黏性後拌入 ③ 料,做成 8 個肉丸置於蒸盤內。

2 水燒開,大火將肉丸蒸 10 分鐘至熟。

3 將調勻的 ④ 料攪拌燒開成糊狀,淋在肉丸上,與麵包配食。

1 Mix ① with ②, mix well until sticky, then mix with ③. Make 8 meatballs and place on steam plate.

2 Boil water, steam meatballs over high heat for 10 minutes until done.

3 Mix ④ well until thickened, drizzle on meatballs, and serve with bread rolls.

1 **⅔ lb. (300g) ground pork**
⅓ lb. (150g) shelled shrimp,
diced

2 **1 egg white**
2 T. ea.: fish sauce, water
¾ t. ea.: sugar, oil, sesame oil
¼ t. pepper, 1 T. cornstarch

3 **1 t. minced garlic**
1 T. chopped green onion

4 **½ c. ea.: diced tomato, water**
1 T. ea.: fish sauce, ketchup
1 t. sugar, 2 t. cornstarch

4 bread rolls

甜酸魚
SWEET AND SOUR FISH

魚 1 條 ....12 兩 [450 公克]
鹽 ....1 小匙
蔥白、薑 [切絲] ....各 1 大匙

① 香菇絲 [見 8 頁] ....2 大匙
  鹹酸菜絲 ....½ 杯
  紅蘿蔔絲 ....¼ 杯

② 番茄絲 ......¼ 杯，水 ....1 杯
  魚露、糖、醋 ....各 1 大匙

③ 水、玉米粉 ....各 1 大匙

④ 蔥綠、辣椒 ....切絲各 ½ 大匙

1 魚洗淨瀝乾，抹鹽醃 20 分鐘，使用前略沖洗，拭乾水份後置於蒸盤。

2 水燒開，將魚放入，大火蒸 15 分鐘 [或微波爐加熱 8 分鐘] 至熟取出。

3 油 2 大匙燒熱，炒香蔥白及薑絲，隨即依序放入 ① 料略炒，再加 ② 料燒開，以調勻的 ③ 料勾芡成薄汁，加 ④ 料，淋在魚上。

1 Wash fish and drain, rub fish with salt and set aside 20 minutes. Wash fish before use, pat dry, then set on a steam plate.

2 Boil water, steam fish over high heat for 15 minutes (or heat in microwave oven 8 minutes); remove when done.

3 Heat 2 T. oil, stir-fry green onion bulb and ginger until fragrant. Add and stir-fry ①, then add ②, bring to boil. Thicken with well-mixed ③, add ④, then drizzle on fish. Serve.

1 whole fish, 1 lb. (450g)
1 t. salt
1 T. ea. (shredded): green onion bulb, ginger root

① **2 T. presoftened Chinese black mushrooms (p. 8), shredded**
  ½ c. shredded pickled mustard cabbage
  ¼ c. shredded carrots

② **¼ c. tomato shreds**
  1 c. water
  1 T. ea.: fish sauce, sugar, vinegar

③ **1 T. ea.: water, cornstarch**

④ **½ T. ea. (shredded): green onion stem, chili pepper**

椰汁燗豬肉
COCONUT SIMMERED PORK

豬蹄膀 ... 2 斤 4 兩 [1350 公克]
蛋 ... 4 個，糖 ... 1 大匙
青椰汁 [或水] ... 5 杯

① 魚露 ... 2 大匙，醬油 ... 3 大匙
  蒜頭 [略拍扁] ... 5 瓣

香菜 ... 隨意

1 雞蛋用水煮熟去殼；蹄膀切塊川燙，洗淨備用。

2 將糖放入乾鍋內，以小火炒呈咖啡色的糖漿 [用意是為了顏色]，再加 ① 料、蛋及蹄膀，煮至肉上色，再加青椰汁 [要蓋滿雞蛋] 煮開，用中小火煮約 30 分鐘，可隨意加香菜。食時配飯加些黃瓜。煮一鍋可分數次享用。

3 lbs. (1350g) pig hocks
4 eggs, 1 T. sugar
5 c. coconut juice or water

① **2 T. fish sauce, 3 T. soy sauce**
  5 garlic cloves, slightly smashed
  coriander as desired

1 Hardboil eggs, remove shells; cut hocks into pieces, blanch, wash, then set aside.

2 With low heat, stir-fry sugar in pan until it becomes brown syrup (sugar used for its color), add ①, eggs and pig hocks, cook until meat changes color. Add coconut juice (must cover eggs), bring to boil, then reduce to medium low heat and cook 30 minutes. Add coriander as desired. Serve with steamed rice and cucumber. May prepare a large portion and serve for several meals.

椰汁燜豬肉 · COCONUT SIMMERED PORK
紅燒魚 · SOUCY FISH

紅燒魚
SOUCY FISH

鯰魚 ... 1 斤 [600 公克]
糖 ... 2 大匙
胡椒 ... ½ 小匙

① 蒜頭 [拍扁] ... 5 瓣
  辣椒 ... 5 支，魚露 ... 4 大匙
  水 ... 3 杯

1 鯰魚洗淨，水燒開，魚放入川燙撈出，將外層白色黏液洗淨再切塊備用。

2 將糖放入乾鍋內，以小火炒呈咖啡色的糖漿 [用意是為了顏色]，隨將 ① 料放入煮滾，再放入魚塊 [水要滿過魚，可多加油豆腐]，湯汁滾後去泡沫，再以中火煮 30 分鐘 [中途翻面]，加上胡椒即可。其汁略鹹除澆飯外，適合與黃瓜配食。

1 ⅓ lbs. (600g) catfish
2 T. sugar
½ t. pepper

① **5 garlic cloves, slightly smashed**
  5 chili peppers, 4 T. fish sauce
  3 c. water

1 Clean catfish, boil water, and blanch catfish. Wash away white film from fish, cut into pieces, then set aside.

2 With low heat, stir-fry sugar in pan until it becomes brown syrup (sugar used for its color), follow with ①, bring to boil. Add fish (water must cover fish and fried bean curd may be added as desired), bring to boil, then remove suds from surface. Reduce heat to medium and cook for 30 minutes (turn over fish at midpoint), add pepper and serve. The slightly salty juice goes well on steamed rice. Serve with cucumber.

生芒果煎魚
FRIED FISH WITH MANGO

魚 1 條 ·············12 兩 [450 公克]
鹽 ·····························½ 小匙
生芒果 [圖 1]·················1 個

1 | 蒜末 ·····························1 小匙
蝦米 [略泡水，切碎]···········1 大匙
辣椒 [切絲]·····················1 小匙

2 | 青檸檬汁····1 大匙，魚露···1 大匙
糖···········1⅓ 小匙，水······2 小匙

1 魚抹上鹽，醃 20 分鐘，使用前略沖洗，拭乾水份。

2 選肉質硬的生芒果，去皮去核取淨重 4 兩 [150 公克] 切粗絲，拌入 1 及 2 料醃 20 分鐘備用。

3 油 3 大匙燒熱，將魚放入煎約 10 分鐘至兩面呈金黃色，取出置盤，上淋醃芒果絲即成。

■ 醃好的芒果絲味酸甜辣又脆，加在煎好的魚上，產生特殊風味，適合與飯配食。若無芒果，將 1 及 2 料混合做為魚的沾料。

1 whole fish, 1 lb. (450g)
½ t. salt
1 young mango (Fig. 1)

1 | **1 t. minced garlic**
1 T. presoftened dried shrimp, chopped
1 t. chili pepper shreds

2 | **1 T. lime juice, 1 T. fish sauce**
1 ⅛ t. sugar, 2 t. water

1 Rub salt on fish, set aside 20 minutes. Wash fish before use, pat dry.

2 Select mango with firm flesh. Remove skin and seed, net weight ⅓ lb. (150g), and cut into thick shreds. Mix in 1 and 2, marinate 20 minutes, and set aside.

3 Heat 3 T. oil, pan-fry fish 10 minutes until both sides are golden brown, and place on plate. Top with marinated mango shreds.

■ The marinated mango shreds taste sour/sweet/spicy and crunchy, bringing a distinct flavor to the fish. Serve with steamed rice. If mango is not available, use sauce made from mixing 1 and 2.

1

香蕉葉蒸魚
FISH STEAMED IN BANANA LEAF

魚肉 [2 公分厚] ·····8 兩 [300 公克]

1 | 鹽 ··········½ 小匙，胡椒······¼ 小匙

2 | 洋菇 [切片]······················2 粒
番茄 ···········2 片，蔥段 ··········4 支
薑絲 ½ 大匙，香茅 [切片]·1 大匙

油····1 小匙，香蕉葉····1½ 尺四方

1 魚拭乾水份，用 1 料醃 20 分鐘。

2 魚置於香蕉葉上 [如葉子不夠大，可數片拼起來用]，2 料平均地擺在魚上，淋入油，包好後再用保鮮膜固定，大火蒸 20 分鐘。若用微波爐，加熱 8 分鐘即可。

■ 越南盛產香蕉，很多香蕉葉被就地取材用於烹飪上，以增添菜餚的風味。

⅔ lb. (300g) fish filet,
(¾", 2 cm thick)

1 | **½ t. salt, ¼ t. pepper**

2 | **2 mushrooms, sliced**
2 tomato slices
4 green onion sections
½ T. shredded ginger root
1 T. lemon grass slices

1 t. oil
1 banana leaf, (18"x18", 45x45cm)

1 Pat dry fish and rub with 1 and let stand for 20 minutes.

2 Place fish on banana leaf (if not large enough, piece several together), spread 2 evenly over fish, drizzle with oil, and wrap with leaf. Secure with plastic wrap and steam over high heat for 20 minutes. If using microwave oven, heat for 8 minutes.

■ Bananas flourish in Vietnam; therefore, banana leaves are incorporated into Vietnamese cooking, giving it an excitingly distinct flavor.

魚漿鑲什蔬
STUFFED VEGETABLES

魚漿[現成已調味] 12 兩[450 公克]
炸豆腐、辣椒、番茄、茄子、長豆
..................共 12 兩[450 公克]

1️⃣
麻油 ....1 小匙
醬油 ....1 大匙
蠔油 ....1 大匙
高湯 [或水] ....¾ 大匙
玉米粉 ....2 小匙

蔥花 ....1 大匙

---

1 炸豆腐、辣椒、番茄切半，茄子切成茄夾；長豆在滾水內川燙立即撈出，泡水後盤捲成圓環；各鑲入魚漿備用。

2 油 6 大匙燒熱，將鑲好的材料魚漿面朝下先煎，兩面各煎 1½ 分鐘至金黃色撈出即可食用。

3 也可將 1️⃣ 料攪拌燒開成薄糊狀，加入蔥花淋在煎好的材料上。可使用的材料廣泛，如苦瓜、香菇、青椒、豆腐等。

■ 辣椒去蕊浸鹽水後會變軟較容易煎，且減少辣味；番茄需去籽；各種材料鑲入魚漿前撒些太白粉，較不會分離。

---

1 lb. (450g) ready-made fish paste
1 lb. (450g) total: fried tofu, chili pepper, tomato, eggplant, long beans

1️⃣
1 t. sesame oil
1 T. ea.: soy sauce, oyster sauce
¾ T. stock (or water)
2 t. cornstarch

1 T. chopped green onion

---

1 Cut fried tofu, chili pepper, and tomato into halves; slice open eggplant to contain filling. Blanch long beans, soak in water, remove, then coil on plate. Fill each with fish paste and set aside.

2 Heat 6 T. oil, pan-fry the fish paste side first, then fry the other side, about 1½ minutes each side until golden brown. Serve.

3 May also mix 1️⃣ well and bring to boil until slightly thickened, add chopped green onion then sprinkle on the fried vegetables. May use other vegetables such as bitter melon, Chinese black mushrooms, bell peppers, and tofu.

■ Soaking deveined chili peppers in salt water makes them easier to cook and reduces the spiciness. Remove seeds from tomatoes. Prior to filling with fish paste, sprinkling cornstarch inside various vegetables helps to secure filling in place.

烤魚
BAKED FISH

魚......................1½ 斤[900 公克]

① 蒜末......................1 小匙
　 紅蔥頭 [切碎]......................1 小匙
　 香茅 [切碎]......................1 小匙
　 魚露......................1 大匙

② 甜醬油 *......................2 大匙
　 油......................3 大匙

③ 絞肉......................4 大匙
　 木耳 [泡過水切碎]......................4 大匙
　 蝦米 [泡水切碎爆香]......................4 大匙
　 炸香紅蔥頭 [見 12 頁]......................4 大匙
　 泡軟冬粉 [切小段]......................½ 杯
　 魚露、鹽......................各 2 小匙
　 胡椒......................½ 小匙
　 蛋 [打散]......................2 大匙

碎花生 [見 12 頁]......................1 大匙

A 式

1 將魚清洗乾淨，拭乾水份，於魚的腹部面由魚嘴向魚尾縱切剖開，魚身兩面每隔 1.5 公分切斜刀 [深至 ⅔ 處]，烤盤內鋪上塗油的鋁鉑紙，將魚背朝上放入。

2 魚的表面塗抹 ① 料醃 2 小時，烤前清除醃料，以防烤時焦黑；魚表面塗上一層油，用鋁鉑紙包好，包時不要緊貼魚身，以避免魚皮脫落。

3 烤箱預熱 375°F [190°C]，烤 20 分鐘後打開鋁鉑紙，再將魚全身塗勻 ② 料，再烤 7 分鐘至魚身呈金黃色，撒上碎花生即可。

B 式

1 魚腹不要剖開，從頭部下面取出內臟，洗淨拭乾；將 ③ 料拌勻填塞入魚肚內。魚身兩面切斜刀 [深至 ⅔ 處]，烤盤內鋪上塗油的鋁鉑紙，將魚背朝上放入。

2、3 做法同於 A 式做法的 **2** 及 **3**，但包鋁鉑紙烤的時間，由 20 分鐘改為 40 分鐘。

＊ 可用"紅燒魚" [見 35 頁] 糖漿的做法代替甜醬油。

■ 本道菜的傳統做法是用炭火烤，吃法可參考 59 頁的"檳海"及"檬"。

---

1 whole fish, 2 lbs. (900g)

① 1 t. minced garlic
　 1 t. minced shallots
　 1 t. minced lemon grass
　 1 T. fish sauce

② 2 T. sweet soy sauce*
　 3 T. oil

③ 4 T. ground pork
　 4 T. presoftened dried wood ears, minced
　 4 T. presoftened dried shrimp, minced and fried
　 4 T. fried shallots (p. 12)
　 ½ c. presoftened bean threads, cut in small sections
　 2 t. fish sauce
　 2 t. salt
　 ½ t. pepper
　 2 T. egg, beaten

1 T. ground roasted peanuts (p. 12)

Style A

1 Wash fish and pat dry, slice open fish belly from chin to tail. Make diagonal incisions ⅔ into flesh every ⅝ inch (1.5cm), place greased foil on baking pan, put fish backside up on foil.

2 Rub ① on fish and marinate 2 hours. Prior to baking, wash away marinade to prevent burning marinade ingredients. Grease fish with oil, loosely wrap with foil to prevent the skin from peeling off.

3 Pre-heat oven to 375°F (190°C), bake 20 minutes, open foil, rub ② evenly on entire fish. Continue baking 7 minutes until fish is golden brown. Sprinkle ground roasted peanuts and serve.

Style B

1 Do not cut open fish belly, remove entrails through gills, wash then pat dry. Stuff well-mixed ③ into fish. Make diagonal incisions ⅔ into flesh on both sides of the fish, place greased foil on baking pan, put fish backside up on foil.

2、3 are the same as steps **2** and **3** in Style A, but baking time for foil-wrapped fish is 40 minutes instead of 20 minutes.

＊ May substitute syrup (see "Fish in Soy Sauce" on p.35) for sweet soy sauce.

■ Barbecuing over charcoal is the traditional way to cook this dish. See p.59 for serving alternatives such as rice noodles and tiny rice sticks.

炒魷魚
STIR-FRIED SQUID

魷魚 [或墨魚]········8 兩 [300 公克]

① 薑 [切絲]·····························1 大匙
蒜 [切碎]·····························1 大匙
泰國檸檬葉 [切絲]···············1 大匙
辣椒絲·································1 小匙

② 魚露································1½ 大匙
白醋································1 小匙
糖································2 小匙

紅、黃椒·················切絲 1½ 大匙

1 魷魚切長方條，每條內面斜劃刀痕，深至 ⅔ 處，轉一方向再斜劃刀痕，成交叉紋並切塊備用。

2 多量水燒開，將切好的魷魚放入川燙，見魷魚捲起即撈出，瀝乾。

3 油 2 大匙燒熱，先炒香 ① 料，再入魷魚略炒，並加入 ② 料及紅、黃椒炒拌均勻即可。

■ 此菜餚與一般炒魷魚方法相同，唯不同的是採用泰國檸檬葉，其味道特殊可口；可使用處理好的冰凍魷魚，極為方便。

⅔ lb. (300g) squid (or cuttlefish)

① 1 T. shredded ginger root
1 T. minced garlic
1 T. shredded kaffir leaf
1 t. shredded chili pepper

② 1 ½ T. fish sauce
1 t. vinegar, 2 t. sugar

1 ½ T. total (shredded): red and yellow bell peppers

1 Cut squid into rectangular strips, make crisscross incisions ⅔ into flesh, cut into pieces and set aside.

2 Boil lots of water, blanch squid pieces, remove when squid curls, and drain.

3 Heat 2 T. oil, stir-fry ① until fragrant, then add squid pieces and stir. Add ② and red and yellow bell peppers; mix evenly and serve.

■ This dish is similar to regular stir-fried squid, the only difference is the kaffir leaf, which gives the dish a distinct exotic flavor. May use prepared frozen squid for convenience.

香茅煎魚
LEMON GRASS FISH (SA CA CHIEN)

石斑魚 2 片 ········12 兩 [450 公克]

① 薑································2 片
蒜································3 瓣
紅蔥頭································2 顆
香茅 [切碎]·····················2 大匙

鹽································¾ 小匙

1 魚洗淨拭乾水份，① 料搗碎加鹽，放入魚內醃 1 小時。

2 油 6 大匙燒熱，用中火將魚煎至兩面微黃肉熟，約 10 分鐘即可。

■ 香茅等料很容易焦，故煎魚時不宜大火，以免燒焦。

2 pieces of red cod, 1 lb. (450g)

① 2 slices ginger root
3 garlic cloves
2 shallots
2 T. chopped lemon grass

¾ t. salt

1 Wash and pat dry fish, mash ① and mix with salt. Marinate fish for 1 hour.

2 Heat 6 T. oil, reduce heat to medium and pan-fry both sides of fish until slightly golden, about 10 minutes.

■ The fish must be pan-fried in medium heat since lemon grass burns easily.

蔗蝦

SHRIMP PASTE ON SUGAR CANE

蝦仁 ····················8 兩 [300 公克]

① 蛋白 ·······················1 個
鹽 ·······················¼ 小匙
糖 ·······················1 小匙
油 ·······················1 小匙
玉米粉 ·······················1 小匙

甘蔗 [12x1.5x1.5 公分] ··········8 支
炸油 ·······················2 杯

1 蝦仁抽腸泥拭乾水份,用刀壓扁剁成泥,加 ① 料仔細用力攪拌至有黏性,冷藏備用。

2 蝦泥分成 8 份,將 1 份蝦泥包裹在甘蔗四週,塗少許油將表面抹光滑。

3 油 2 杯燒熱,中火將蔗蝦煎炸 5 分鐘至表面呈金黃色即可。蔗蝦可當前菜。其他吃法可參考 59 頁的"檳海"及"檬"。

■ 傳統做法中,蝦泥內多加入蒸熟的肥豬肉[切碎粒],不喜油者可以不加。甘蔗本身有甜味,加上蝦的煎炸鮮味,在丟棄之前,不妨啃一啃,吸食其中的精華。

■ 可使用罐裝甘蔗十分方便。

⅔ lb. (300g) shelled shrimp

1 egg white
¼ t. salt
① 1 t. sugar
1 t. oil
1 t. cornstarch

8 sugar cane pieces, 5" (12cm) long
2 c. oil for deep-frying

1 Devein shrimp and pat dry. Flatten with knife blade, chop, and mash into paste. Add ① and mix well until sticky. Refrigerate.

2 Divide shrimp paste into 8 portions. Cover entire sugar cane with one portion shrimp paste and glaze surface with oil.

3 Heat 2 c. oil, deep-fry sugar cane in medium heat for 5 minutes until golden brown. "Shrimp paste on sugar cane" may be served as an appetizer. See p.59 for serving alternatives such as rice noodles and tiny rice sticks.

■ In traditional cooking, add steamed pork fat (diced) to shrimp paste. Fat is optional as desired. Sugar cane tastes naturally sweet; flavor is enhanced by the fried shrimp, and is delicious to gnaw on prior to discarding.

■ Canned sugar cane is convenient to use.

香露大頭蝦
FRAGRANT GIANT SHRIMP

6 人份 · Serves 6

大頭蝦 3 隻 ……… 1½ 斤 [900 公克]

①
魚露 ………………………………… 2 大匙
水 ……………………………………… 2 杯
糖 ………………………………… 4 小匙

蔥花 ………………………………… 2 大匙
炸油 ………………………………… 適量

1 蝦洗淨瀝乾，由背部切開分為二，抽出腸泥，撒玉米粉在蝦肉上，蝦頭須要多撒些 [可用篩子撒粉以求均勻]。

2 炸油燒熱，放入蝦，煎炸至熟。為避免頭部的蝦黃散開，蝦殼面宜向下，油蓋滿過蝦可免翻轉。

3 將 ① 料燒開，放入煎熟的蝦，煮約 3 分鐘使入味，放入蔥花即可。

■ 大頭蝦是一種淡水蝦，在越南盛產。因頭部有很多蝦黃，且蝦肉味鮮而受歡迎。

3 giant shrimp (tom cang),
  2 lbs. (900g)

①
2 T. fish sauce
2 c. water
4 t. sugar

2 T. chopped green onions
oil for deep-frying

1 Wash and pat dry shrimp, cut from back to belly into halves, devein, and sprinkle cornstarch on shrimp. Shrimp heads require more cornstarch (may use sifter to sprinkle evenly).

2 Heat oil for deep-frying, fry shrimp until done. To prevent shrimp heads from disintegrating, place shrimps' back toward bottom of pot. Shrimp immersed in oil do not require turning over.

3 Bring ① to boil, add fried shrimp, and cook 3 minutes. Add chopped green onions and serve.

■ These fresh water giant shrimp are found largely in Vietnam and other parts of Southeast Asia. They are very popular among the Vietnamese because of their freshness and the large amount of eggs found in them.

啤酒蟹
BEER CRAB

活蟹 1 隻..............1 斤 [600 公克]

1
蔥..4 支
薑..4 片
啤酒 1 罐............9 兩 [340 公克]

2
青檸檬汁..............................2 大匙
鹽、胡椒......................各 1/8 小匙
辣椒..隨意

1 live crab, 1 1/3 lbs. (600g)

1
4 green onions
4 ginger root slices
12 oz. (340g) beer

2
2 T. lime juice
1/8 t. salt
1/8 t. pepper
chili pepper as desired

1 蟹洗淨外殼，打開蟹蓋，去除鰓及蟹蓋嘴上的胃袋，將蟹殼刷洗乾淨，再蓋上蟹蓋連同 ① 料放入鍋內，煮滾後蓋鍋，大火煮 10 分鐘至蟹肉熟；② 料調勻做為沾料。

2 蟹剁塊，沾 ② 料食用。冷食熱食均可。

■ 凡是帶殼的海產，如蝦、蜆等都可用此方法，快又簡便，煮蟹湯汁可拿來蒸蛋。

1 Wash crab shell, pry open shell from body, and remove gills and other innards from shell. Scrub and wash inside of shell, then cover on crab body. Put crab with ① into pot, bring to boil, cover and cook 10 minutes over high heat until done. Mix ② well to make dipping sauce.

2 Cut crab into pieces, serve with ② sauce. This dish can be served cold or hot.

■ All shellfish such as shrimp and clams may be prepared as above, fast and easy. The cooked crab broth may be used in steaming eggs.

燜蛤蜊
SIMMERED CLAMS

蛤蜊 [蜆]..............1 斤 [600 公克]

1
鹽..1/2 小匙
香菜 [切碎]..........................1 大匙
蒜、辣椒 [切碎]..............各 1/2 小匙
紅蔥頭 [切碎]......................1 大匙
青檸檬汁..............................1 大匙
番茄丁......................................3/4 杯

1 1/3 lbs. (600g) live clams

1
1/2 t. salt
1 T. minced coriander
1/2 t. ea.(minced): garlic, chili
**   pepper**
1 T. minced shallots
3/4 c. chopped tomatoes
1 T. lime juice

1 將蛤蜊逐一刷洗備用。① 料備在容器內做為沾料。

2 水 1 杯燒開放入蛤蜊，蓋鍋燒開後，逐一取出開口的蛤蜊，沾 ① 料或 "甜酸辣魚露沾料" 食用。

■ 蛤蜊開口即熟，煮過久太老就不好吃。一般均用炒的方式烹調蛤蜊，但採用這種做法簡單好吃，受人歡迎。

1 Scrub and wash clams; set aside. Prepare ① in a container for dipping.

2 Boil 1 c. water, put in clams, cover and bring to boil. Immediately remove all opened clams, serve with ① sauce or "sweet/sour/spicy fish sauce".

■ Opened clams indicate doneness; over-cooked clams taste rubbery. Stir-frying is a common way to cook clams, but the above dish is popular because it is easy and tasty.

炸軟殼蟹
FRIED SOFT SHELL CRAB (CUA LOT VO)

冷凍軟殼蟹 3 隻 ·12 兩 [450 公克]
麵粉 ....1 杯
炸油 ....適量

1 軟殼蟹解凍後，洗淨外殼，在蟹眼睛的兩側掀開小縫，小心地除去鰓及蟹蓋嘴上方之胃袋，並拭乾水份。

2 將蟹逐一放入麵粉內輕拍，並掀開蟹蓋的左右兩側均勻地撒上麵粉。

3 多量油燒熱，放入蟹，油保持中溫，將蟹炸 8 分鐘至兩面香酥，撈出瀝乾油。炸好的蟹，可連殼食用。

■ 蟹要買大隻的，炸時油量要多，冷凍蟹帶鹹味，不需加調味。可依個人喜好沾青檸檬汁。

■ 如果買到活的軟殼蟹，則炸出來的顏色更佳，味道更鮮美。

**3 frozen soft shell crabs,
    1 lb. (450g)
1 c. flour
oil for deep-frying**

1 After thawing crabs, wash shells, pry open the two small slits on both sides of the crabs' eyes, carefully remove the gills and other innards from shell, then pat dry.

2 Put crabs into flour and tap lightly; pry open the shells and sprinkle flour evenly on both sides.

3 Heat a lot of oil, place crabs into oil, and maintain oil temperature at medium heat. Fry crabs 8 minutes until both sides are crispy; remove and drain. The fried crabs including the shells may be served.

■ Buy larger crabs; use plenty of oil for frying. Frozen crabs taste slightly salty; additional salt is not needed. May use lime juice as desired.

■ If live soft shell crabs are available, the fried soft shell crabs yield an even more brilliant color and delicious flavor.

鰍魚 ....8 兩 [300 公克]	

①	酸子 [見 6 頁] ....3 大匙 水 [或高湯] ....5 杯
②	魚露.................2 大匙，糖 ....1 大匙
③	拔哈 [bac ha] [或西芹] 撕皮切段 ....1 杯 番茄、鳳梨 [切塊].................共 1 杯
④	豆芽菜.................2 杯 五芥、五汪 *[或蔥花]切碎共 4 大匙 生辣椒 [斜切片].................1 支

鰍魚酸湯
SOUR CATFISH SOUP

1 水燒開，先將鰍魚川燙撈出，把外層白色黏液洗淨再切塊。

2 將 ① 料煮滾，熄火蓋鍋 5 分鐘，見酸子軟了，瀝出渣，湯汁備用。

3 把 ① 料湯汁燒開，放入魚塊再燒開，依序加入 ② 及 ③ 料煮開，再加 ④ 料即可上桌。此為道地的越南開胃湯。

■ 可用雞或蝦取代魚肉。市場有售瓶裝或袋裝"越式酸湯調味料"，使用方便。

★ 五芥、五汪 [圖 1]

1 catfish, ⅖ lb. (300g)	

①	**3 T. tamarind (p. 7)** **5 c. water (or stock)**
②	**2 T. fish sauce, 1 T. sugar**
③	**1 c. bac ha (or celery), peeled and sectioned** **1 c. total (cut in pieces): tomato, pineapple**
④	**2 c. bean sprouts** **4 T. total (chopped): ngo gai*, ngo om* (or green onions)** **1 chili pepper, cut diagonally**

1 Boil water and blanch catfish. Wash away white film from fish, cut into pieces.

2 Bring ① to boil, turn off heat and cover 5 minutes. When tamarind is softened, strain and discard pulp, set aside broth.

3 Bring ① broth to boil, put in fish pieces and bring to boil again. Add ② and ③ then bring to boil; add ④ and serve. This dish is an authentic Vietnamese appetizer soup.

■ May use chicken or shrimp instead of fish. Markets sell canned or bagged "Vietnamese sour soup mix" that are convenient to use.

★ See Fig.1 for ngo gai, ngo om.

①	夾心豬肉 ....4 兩 [150 公克] 蝦米 [泡水].................¼ 杯
②	罐頭筍 [切片川燙]·4 兩 [150 公克] 鹹酸菜 [切塊].................4 兩 [150 公克]
	魚露 ....1 小匙

酸菜筍片湯
BAMBOO AND PICKLED CABBAGE SOUP

1 水 6 杯燒滾，放入 ① 料，煮開去除泡沫，以小火煮 20 分鐘熄火，泡 15 分鐘，肉取出切薄片。

2 肉湯內放入 ② 料，湯滾後再煮 5 分鐘加魚露，起鍋前加肉片即可。酸菜有鹹味，先試鹹淡再加魚露。

■ 若用豬腳或豬骨 12 兩 [450 公克]取代豬肉，需先與蝦米煮 50 分鐘，再加 ② 料，此為家庭常做的開胃湯。

①	**⅓ lb. (150g) pork*** **¼ c. presoftened dried shrimp**
②	**⅓ lb. (150g) canned bamboo shoots, sliced and blanched** **⅓ lb. (150g) pickled mustard cabbage, cut in pieces**
	1 t. fish sauce

1 Bring 6 c. water to boil, add ① and boil, remove suds. Reduce heat to low and cook 20 minutes. Turn off heat and let set 15 minutes. Remove and cut pork into thin slices.

2 Put ② into broth; after bringing broth to boil, cook for an additional 5 minutes. Add fish sauce. Add sliced pork just prior to removing from heat. The pickled mustard cabbage is already salty; taste soup before adding fish sauce.

★ Use pork containing fat for best flavor.

■ If using 1 lb. (450g) pig's feet or pork bones instead of pork, must first cook with presoftened dried shrimp for 50 minutes, then add ②. This appetizing soup makes a frequent appearance in family style meals.

1

蟹肉魚肚羹
CRAB MEAT PIKE MAW SOUP

魚肚 [圖 1]················2 條
蟹肉 [罐裝或冷凍]···············½ 杯

1 | 高湯 [見 9 頁] 4 杯，魚露·1 大匙

2 | 玉米粉、水 ···············各 2 大匙

3 | 鹽、胡椒 ···············各 ¼ 小匙
   | 酒 ···············1 大匙

2 fried conger pike maw (Fig. 1)
½ c. crab meat (canned or
**   frozen)**

1 | **4 c. stock (p. 9), 1 T. fish sauce**

2 | **2 T. cornstarch, 2 T. water**

3 | **¼ t. salt**
   | **¼ t. pepper**
   | **1 T. cooking wine**

1 多量水燒開，將魚肚煮軟，撈出擠乾水份，切 2.5 公分長。

2 將 ① 料燒開，放入魚肚及蟹肉後再燒開，以調勻的 ② 料勾芡成薄汁，加 ③ 料。亦可隨喜好加紅醋[見 6 頁]。

■ 選擇色白及沙爆的魚肚較佳，也需有好的高湯搭配。魚肚含有膠質，故滑潤順口。可用白木耳及干貝，取代魚肚及蟹肉。

1 Boil a lot of water, cook fried conger pike maw until softened, remove and squeeze out water. Cut into 1 inch (2.5cm) lengths.

2 Bring ① to boil, add fried conger pike maw and crab meat, then bring to boil again. Slightly thicken with well-mixed ②, add ③. As desired, may add red vinegar (p.6).

■ White and sand-fried conger pike maw is best; also must use tasty stock to bring out its flavor. Because fried conger pike maw has a sticky consistency, it tastes wonderfully soft and pliant. May substitute white wood ears and scallops for fried conger pike maw and crab meat.

---

1 | 白蘆筍 * [切半] ···············1 杯
   | 金針菇 [切除根部]···············½ 杯
   | 火腿 [切絲]···············⅓ 杯
   | 以上共 6 兩 [225 公克]

2 | 高湯 [見 9 頁] 4 杯，薑末·1 小匙
   | 魚露 ·······1 大匙，鹽·········⅛ 小匙

3 | 玉米粉 ···3 大匙，水 ·········3 大匙

   香菜、蔥 ···············切碎共 1 大匙

蘆筍金針菇湯
ASPARAGUS AND MUSHROOM SOUP

1 先將 ② 料煮開，以調勻的 ③ 料勾芡成薄汁，再入 ① 料煮開。最後再撒上香菜、蔥花即成。

★ 本食譜使用罐頭蘆筍，也可用新鮮蘆筍。

■ 這是一道簡易、家喻戶曉且極受歡迎的外來家常菜。

1 | **½ lb. (225g) total:**
   | **1 c. white asparagus*,**
   | **   cut in half**
   | **½ c. golden mushrooms,**
   | **   roots removed**
   | **⅓ c. shredded ham**

2 | **4 c. stock (p. 9)**
   | **1 t. minced ginger root**
   | **1 T. fish sauce, ⅛ t. salt**

3 | **3 T. cornstarch, 3 T. water**

   1 T. total (chopped):
   **   coriander, green onion**

1 Bring ② to boil, slightly thicken broth with well-mixed ③, add ① and bring to boil again. Add coriander and green onion; serve.

★ This recipe calls for canned asparagus; may also use fresh asparagus.

■ This is an easy, well-known, and highly popular home style dish with foreign influence.

1

拌木瓜絲
SHREDDED PAPAYA SALAD

2 人份 · Serves 2

①
生木瓜絲… 8 兩 [300 公克]
甜豬肉乾絲… ¼ 杯
九層塔切絲… 1 杯，碎花生… 2 大匙

②
紅醋 [見 6 頁]… 3 大匙
辣椒醬… 1 大匙，鹽… ¼ 小匙
糖… 2 大匙，水… 2 大匙

1 將 ① 料置盤，食時依各人口味酌量拌入 ② 料即可。此道菜可當零嘴或小菜。

①
- ⅔ lb. (300g) fresh papaya, shredded
- ¼ c. sweetened pork jerky, shredded
- 1 c. fresh basil, shredded
- 2 T. ground roasted peanuts (p. 12)

②
- 3 T. red rice vinegar (p. 6)
- 1 T. chili paste, ¼ t. salt
- 2 T. ea.: sugar, water

1 Place ① on a plate, while serving mix in ② (adjust amount of each item as desired). This dish may be served as a snack or an appetizer.

雞絲沙拉
SHREDDED CHICKEN SALAD (GOI CA)

2 人份 · Serves 2

①
雞腿 1 隻… 12 兩 [450 公克]
高麗菜、香草葉…共 8 兩 [300 公克]

碎花生 [見 12 頁]… 1 大匙
甜酸辣魚露沾料 [見 13 頁]…適量

1 將雞腿煮 [或蒸] 熟去皮去骨，肉撕成絲，① 料切絲。

2 雞肉絲與 ① 料翻拌，放入盤內，撒上碎花生，再隨意淋上 "甜酸辣魚露沾料"。沙拉內可任意搭配蝦仁、扎肉、其他肉類或蔬菜。

①
- 1 chicken leg, 1 lb. (450g)
- ⅔ lb. (300g) total: cabbage, fragrant spices/herbs

- 1 T. ground roasted peanuts (p. 12)
- sweet/sour/spicy fish sauce (p. 13) as desired

1 Boil or steam chicken leg until done. Remove skin and bone; shred.

2 Mix shredded chicken with ①, place on a plate, sprinkle ground roasted peanuts, and drizzle "sweet/sour/spicy fish sauce" as desired. Cooked shrimp, Vietnamese meat loaf, other meats or vegetables may be added as desired.

蒜茸空心菜
MINCED GARLIC ON-CHOY

2 人份 · Serves 2

空心菜 [切段]… 8 兩 [300 公克]
魚露… 2 大匙

①
蒜末… 1 大匙
辣椒 [切碎]… 1 小匙

1 油 3 大匙燒熱，先將 ① 料炒香，隨入空心菜及魚露大火炒 [若火力不強，放入空心菜，隨即蓋鍋約 1 分鐘，等溫度提升後再翻拌，效果奇佳]，炒出的空心菜脆綠可口。也可以將菜燙熟，沾魚露加青檸檬汁及辣椒。

- ⅔ lb. (300g) on-choy, sectioned
- 2 T. fish sauce

①
- 1 T. minced garlic
- 1 t. chopped chili pepper

1 Heat 3 T. oil, stir-fry ① until fragrant, add on-choy and fish sauce; stir-fry with high heat (if the heat is not high enough, after adding on-choy, immediately cover 1 minute. After heat increases, then stir; this achieves a similar result). This stir-fried vegetable appears bright green and tastes crispy and delicious. May also quick-boil the on-choy, then serve with mixed fish sauce, lime juice, and chili pepper.

蒜茸空心菜 • MINCED GARLIC ON-CHOY
蝦米炒涼薯 • STIR-FRIED SHRIMP AND YIMACA

蝦米炒涼薯
STIR-FRIED SHRIMP AND YIMACA

2 人份 · Serves 2

①
蝦米 [泡水]… ¼ 杯
鹽… ¼ 小匙，魚露… 1 小匙

②
涼薯 [沙葛]、木耳及其他蔬菜均切絲…共 8 兩 [300 公克]

1 油 2 大匙燒熱，先炒香蝦米，隨入 ① 料及 ② 料炒拌均勻即可。涼薯脆脆甜甜的，與豆腐乾或任何蔬菜搭配均好吃。

①
- ¼ c. presoftened dried shrimp
- ¼ t. salt
- 1 t. fish sauce

②
- ⅔ lb. (300g) total (shredded): yimaca, dried wood ears, and other desired vegetables

1 Heat 2 T. oil, stir-fry dried shrimp until fragrant, add ① and ②, mix thoroughly and serve. Yimaca tastes crunchy and sweet, suitable to serve with pressed bean curd or any vegetables.

春捲檳海
TINY RICE STICKS WITH EGG ROLLS

① 越式春捲‥‥‥‥‥‥‥‥‥‥[見 77 頁]
　 蔗蝦‥‥‥‥‥‥‥‥‥‥‥‥[見 45 頁]
　 烤肉丸串、烤豬肉串‥‥‥‥[見 31 頁]
　 任意選一或數種‥‥‥‥‥共 16 卷[串]

　 檳 [最細]‥‥‥‥‥‥4 兩 [150 公克]
　 生菜‥‥‥‥‥‥‥‥‥‥‥‥24 片

② 任選香草葉 [見 12 頁]‥‥‥‥‥3 杯
　 酸甜紅白蘿蔔絲 [見 13 頁]‥‥‥1 杯
　 黃瓜切片‥‥‥‥‥‥‥‥‥‥2 杯

　 甜酸辣魚露沾料 [見 13 頁]‥‥‥2 杯

③ 油蔥 [見 12 頁]‥‥‥‥‥‥‥2 大匙
　 碎花生 [見 12 頁]‥‥‥‥‥‥4 大匙

　 生菜，米紙 [小]‥‥‥‥‥各 16 張

1 檳泡水 20 分鐘，瀝乾。

2 水燒開，放入檳，待水滾爛 2 分鐘後，再 1 份 1 份撈出盤捲成 1 團團。講究者則撈出後薄薄地鋪在盤上，冷後依所需大小剪開成方塊。食前撒上 ③ 料即成"檳海"。

3 "檳海"放在生菜上，隨意加入 ① 料，再加 ② 料後用米紙包捲，沾上"甜酸辣魚露沾料"食用。

春捲檳　碗內放入煮好的檳[粗細隨意]、生菜[撕小片]、① 料、② 料及 ③ 料，隨意拌入"甜酸辣魚露沾料"即可食用。

■ 此為極有代表性的越南菜餚，無論是在家庭或餐廳均普遍受歡迎。

---

① **16 of the following single
　 ingredient or assorted
　 combination:
　 Shrimp Paste on Sugar Cane
　 (p. 45)
　 Fried Egg Rolls (p. 77)
　 Skewered Charbroiled
　 Meatballs (p. 31)
　 Skewered Charbroiled Pork
　 (p. 31)**

**⅛ lb. (150g) thinnest rice
　 noodles
24 lettuce leaves**

② **3 c. any fragrant spices/herbs
　 (p. 12)
1 c. sweet/sour carrots and
　 turnips (p. 13)
2 c. sliced cucumber**

**2 c. sweet/sour/spicy fish
　 sauce (p. 13)**

③ **2 T. fried green onions (p. 12)
4 T. ground roasted peanuts
　 (p. 12)**

**16 lettuce leaves
16 sheets of rice paper (small)**

1 Soak rice noodles 20 minutes, drain.

2 Boil water, then add the noodles. After boiling, simmer 2 minutes. Scoop and drain one portion at a time, then coil into mounds. For those who insist on correct form, after scooping out the noodles, spread them thinly on a plate. Let cool, then trim lengths to make a square. Sprinkle ③ and serve; this is "tiny rice sticks".

3 Place the rice sticks on lettuce, add ① as desired then ②, wrap with rice paper. Dip in "sweet/sour/spicy fish sauce" and serve.

Rice Noodles with Egg Rolls In a bowl place cooked rice noodles (select thickness as desired), lettuce (small torn pieces), ingredients ①, ②, and ③; drizzle with "sweet/sour/spicy fish sauce" as desired and serve.

■ This favorite is one of the most popular classic Vietnamese dishes. It is frequently served and very welcome in most families and restaurants.

什錦河粉
FRIED RICE NOODLES (PHO AP CHAO)

1　河粉買來先用手一條一條鬆開，攤平放在盤內，若不急用，攤平後先放冰箱冷藏。多量水燒開，分別將 ① 各料燙熟撈出。

2　油 1 大匙燒熱，放入河粉先略煎再搖動鍋子以免焦黑，呈金黃色再翻面，黏鍋時由鍋邊加油，中火兩面共煎 5 分鐘[用不黏鍋較易煎]。置盤上。

3　油 2 大匙燒熱，將 ② 各料依序放入，翻炒至肉熟，隨即加 ③ 及調勻的 ④ 料，炒拌燒開成薄糊狀，再入燙熟的 ① 料燒開，淋在河粉上即成。

★ 切法見 43 頁 "炒魷魚" 做法 1 。

| ① | 蝦··········4 隻，鮮魷魚 *··8 片 |
| | 油菜 [切段] 1 杯，紅蘿蔔·······8 片 |

新鮮條狀河粉·····12 兩 [450 公克]

| ② | 豬肉····8 片，洋蔥 [切片]····¼ 杯 |
| | 洋菇 [切半]·················4 個 |

| ③ | 魚丸·········4 粒，番茄········6 片 |

④	蠔油····2 大匙，玉米粉·····1 大匙
	鹽··········¼ 小匙，水········1 杯
	糖、醋·················各 1 小匙

① 4 shrimp, 8 squid slices*
1 c. yu choy, sectioned
8 carrot slices

1 lb. (450g) fresh rice noodles

② 8 pork slices
¼ c. onion slices
4 mushrooms, cut in half

③ 4 fish balls
6 tomato slices

④ 2 T. oyster sauce
1 T. cornstarch
¼ t. salt
1 c. water
1 t. ea: sugar, vinegar

1 Remove fresh rice noodles from package and loosen each noodle by hand. Spread noodles flat on a plate. If not in a hurry, refrigerate after spreading them flat. Boil a lot of water, separately blanch each ingredient in ①; remove.

2 Heat 1 T. oil, lightly pan-fry the fresh rice noodles, and shake pan to prevent burning. Turn over noodles when one side appears golden. If they stick to the pan, add oil at side of pan. Pan-fry both sides of noodles with medium heat, a total of 5 minutes (it is easier to use a non-stick pan). Set on a plate.

3 Heat 2 T. oil, add ingredients in ② in order, stir-fry until pork is cooked; immediately add ③ and well-mixed ④, stir-fry until boiling and slightly thickened; then add quick-boiled ingredients in ①, bring to boil and pour over fresh rice noodles. Serve.

★ See p.43, procedure 1 in "Stir-fried Squid" on how to cut squid.

什錦炒麵
FRIED EGG NOODLES

1　將蛋麵鬆開放入多量滾水內燙 10 秒鐘，立即撈出瀝乾，攤平於盤內。

2、3　做法同上 2 及 3 。

蒸熟蛋麵·············6 兩 [225 公克]

①②③④ 料同上

½ lb. (225g) ready-steamed egg noodles

①②③④ same as above recipe

1 Loosen egg noodles and place in a lot of boiling water for 10 seconds; immediately remove and drain; spread noodles flat on a plate. Other ingredients and procedures are the same as above.

2、3 see procedures 2 and 3 of the above recipe.

炒豆飯
FRIED RICE WITH LONG BEANS

乾干貝 [圖 1]·············2 個
香腸·······················2 條
① 米、水 [含泡干貝水]·····各 1 杯
鹽·······················⅛ 小匙

長豆 [切丁]·········4 兩 [150 公克]
魚露·····················1½ 大匙

2 dried scallops (Fig. 1)

**2 sausages
① 1 c. rice, ⅛ t. salt
1 c. water (including scallop
water)**

**⅓ lb. (150g) long beans, diced
1 ½ T. fish sauce**

1 干貝用 ½ 杯的溫水泡 1 小時至軟，撈出撕成絲，湯汁留用。干貝絲連同 ① 料放入電鍋內煮至米熟，香腸取出切丁[¾ 杯]，放回飯鍋內。

2 油 1 大匙燒熱，大火把長豆略炒，隨入魚露炒拌，鏟出與煮好的飯趁熱翻拌均勻即可。

■ 此道菜做法簡單，長豆脆綠，香腸帶甜味非常可口，若無香腸可用火腿取代。

1 Soak dried scallops in ½ c. warm water for 1 hour until softened, remove and shred; set aside scallop water. Place shredded scallops and ① in electric rice cooker and cook until rice is done. Remove sausages and dice (¾ c.), return diced sausages to rice cooker.

2 Heat 1 T. oil, slightly stir-fry long beans with high heat, add fish sauce and stir. Scoop out and mix thoroughly with warm cooked rice and serve.

■ This very tasty dish is easy to make, with lush green, crunchy long beans and slightly sweet sausages. If sausages are not available, may use ham.

海 南 雞 飯
HAINAN CHICKEN RICE

雞 ½ 隻·············1 斤 [600 公克]

① 鹽····1 小匙，蔥 [切段拍扁]····3 支
米·········1 杯，蒜末·······1 小匙

② 薑 [磨碎]、蒜末···········各 1 小匙
糖、醋、魚露、水········各 2 小匙

酸甜紅白蘿蔔絲 [見 13 頁]····適量

½ chicken, 1 ⅓ lbs. (600g)

**1 t. salt
① 3 green onions, sectioned and
slightly smashed**

1 c. rice, 1 t. minced garlic

**1 t. minced ginger root
② 1 t. minced garlic
2 t. ea: sugar, vinegar
fish sauce, water**

**sweet/sour carrots and turnips
(p. 13) as desired**

1 將 ① 料抹在雞表面，醃 2 小時；米泡水 2 小時後瀝乾；② 料拌勻當沾料。

2 水 10 杯燒開，將雞連蔥放入燒開，續煮 20 分鐘後熄火，蓋鍋燜 20 分鐘後取出剁塊備用。

3 油 1 大匙燒熱，炒香蒜末，隨即放入泡好的米，中火炒 3 分鐘後加入煮雞的湯 1½ 杯，放入電鍋煮成飯。

4 盤內盛飯，放入雞塊、黃瓜及 "酸甜紅白蘿蔔絲"。食時雞塊沾沾料。

1 Rub ① on chicken, marinate 2 hours; soak rice in water 2 hours, drain; mix ② thoroughly as dipping sauce.

2 Boil 10 c. water, add chicken and green onions, bring to boil. Continue cooking 20 minutes and turn off heat. Cover and simmer 20 minutes, then remove chicken and cut into pieces.

3 Heat 1 T. oil, stir-fry minced garlic until fragrant, followed by pre-soaked rice; stir-fry with medium heat 3 minutes, then add 1½ c. cooked chicken broth, place in rice cooker and cook until done.

4 Scoop rice on to a plate, add cut chicken pieces, cucumber, and "sweet/sour carrots and turnips". While serving, dip chicken pieces in dipping sauce.

雲吞麵
WON TON NOODLES

2 人份・ Serves 2

1	絞肉 ⋯⋯⋯⋯⋯⋯⋯4 兩 [150 公克] 炸乾大地魚 *[圖 1，切碎] ⋯1 大匙 鹽、胡椒 ⋯⋯⋯⋯⋯各 ⅛ 小匙 麻油 ⋯⋯⋯⋯⋯⋯⋯⋯⋯¼ 小匙 水 ⋯⋯1 大匙，玉米粉 ⋯⋯2 小匙
	雲吞皮 24 張，麵·4 兩 [150 公克]
2	叉燒肉或熟豬肉 ⋯⋯⋯⋯⋯⋯8 片 香菜、蔥 ⋯⋯⋯⋯⋯切碎各 ¼ 杯
3	高湯 [見 9 頁] ⋯⋯⋯⋯⋯⋯5 杯 鹽 ⋯¾ 小匙，糖 ⋯⋯⋯⋯2 小匙 魚露 ⋯⋯1 大匙，胡椒 ⋯⋯⋯隨意

1 將 ① 料仔細攪拌，分成 24 份，用雲吞皮包成雲吞 [僅用 12 個雲吞，剩餘的留下次用]。① 料內的紋肉可隨喜好混入 ½ 杯蝦或蟹肉。

2 大量水燒開，將麵依包裝指示煮熟，雲吞煮到浮起，分別盛於 2 碗內，擺入 ② 料。

3 把 ③ 料燒滾，隨即加在煮好的麵及雲吞上，即成。

* 即曬乾的大地魚用油炸過，主要用來增加菜餚的香味。

1	⅓ lb. (150g) ground pork 1 T. deep-fried dried red 　snapper* (Fig. 1), chopped ⅛ t. ea.: salt, pepper ¼ t. sesame oil 1 T. water, 2 t. cornstarch
	24 sheets of won ton skin ⅓ lb. (150g) noodles
2	8 slices barbecued or cooked 　pork ¼ c. ea. (chopped): coriander, 　green onions
3	5 c. stock (p. 9), ¾ t. salt 2 t. sugar, 1 T. fish sauce pepper as desired

1 Mix ① thoroughly and divide mixture into 24 portions, wrap with won ton skin (use only 12 won tons; save the remainder for future use). The ground pork in ingredients ① may be mixed with ½ c. shrimp or crab meat as desired.

2 Boil a lot of water, cook noodles according to cooking instructions on package, cook won tons until they float to the top; divide noodles and won tons into two bowls, add ②.

3 Bring ③ to boil, then pour soup on noodles and won tons; serve.

* The main purpose of deep-frying sun-dried red snapper is to enhance flavor.

美萩 (美拖) 粿條
TAPIOCA STICKS

2 人份・ Serves 2

1	豆芽菜 ⋯⋯⋯⋯⋯⋯⋯⋯⋯⋯⋯1 杯 美萩粿條 [圖 2] ⋯⋯4 兩 [150 公克]
1	高湯 [見 9 頁] ⋯5 杯，鹽 ⋯¾ 小匙 糖 ⋯⋯2 小匙，魚露 ⋯⋯⋯2 大匙
2	叉燒肉或熟豬肉 ⋯⋯⋯⋯⋯⋯8 片 熟蝦 ⋯⋯4 隻，魚丸 ⋯⋯⋯4 粒 熟蟹箝 ⋯⋯⋯⋯⋯⋯⋯⋯⋯2 隻
3	生菜 ⋯⋯1 片，韭菜 [切段] ⋯⋯5 支 芹菜 [切碎] ⋯⋯⋯⋯⋯⋯⋯1 大匙 炸香紅蔥頭 [見 12 頁] ⋯⋯⋯½ 小匙

1 豆芽菜分盛 2 碗，粿條煮熟 [見 11 頁]，置於豆芽菜上。

2 將 ① 料燒滾，② 料分別在 ① 料內燙熱後連同 ③ 料置於粿條上，再加入煮滾的 ① 料即成。

1	1 c. bean sprouts ⅓ lb. (150g) tapioca sticks 　(Fig. 2)
1	5 c. stock (p. 9), ¾ t. salt 2 t. sugar, 2 T. fish sauce
2	8 cooked or barbecued pork 　slices 4 cooked shrimp, 4 fish balls 2 cooked crab claws
3	1 lettuce leaf 5 Chinese chives, sectioned 1 T. celery, chopped ½ t. fried shallots (p. 12)

1 Fill two separate bowls with bean sprouts. Cook tapioca sticks until done (p.11) and place on bean sprouts.

2 Bring ① to boil. Separately quick-cook each item of ② in ①; remove and place with ③ on tapioca sticks. Add boiling hot ①; serve.

豬腳瀨粉
PIG'S FEET WITH RICE NOODLES

豬腳或蹄膀⋯⋯⋯⋯1½ 斤 [900 公克]

① 蝦米⋯⋯⋯⋯¼ 杯，水⋯⋯⋯⋯20 杯

② 魚露⋯⋯⋯1 大匙，鹽⋯⋯⋯¾ 小匙

瀨粉 [圖 1]⋯⋯⋯⋯12 兩 [450 公克]

③ 香菜、蔥⋯⋯⋯⋯切碎共 2 大匙
胡椒、辣椒、青檸檬汁⋯⋯⋯隨意

2 lbs. (900g) pig's feet or hocks

① **¼ c. dried shrimp, 20 c. water**

② **1 T. fish sauce, ¾ t. salt**

1 lb. (450g) Vietnamese rice noodles (Fig. 1)

③ **2 T. total (chopped): coriander, green onions**
pepper , chili pepper, lime juice as desired

1 豬腳剁塊，放入多量的滾水內川燙，連同 ① 料煮開後，改用中火煮約 50 分鐘或煮到喜歡的軟度。因燒煮時間長，1 次煮 1½ 斤，剩下的豬腳及高湯可留下次食用。

2 取煮好的高湯 5 杯及適量豬腳燒開，瀨粉在熱水內川燙撈出，放入豬腳湯內煮開，加 ② 料分盛 2 碗，食時隨喜好加入 ③ 料。

■ 瀨粉在豬腳湯內煮過後，非常入味且柔滑可口，對老人或小孩很適宜。

1 Cut pig's feet into pieces, blanch in plenty of boiling water, bring to boil with ①. Reduce heat to medium and cook 50 minutes or until desired doneness. Because cooking time is extensive, preparing 2 lb. at one time allows for future use of pig's feet and stock.

2 Bring to boil 5 c. stock and desired amount of pig's feet. Blanch Vietnamese rice noodles and put into soup with the pig's feet pieces; bring to boil. Add ② and separately put into 2 bowls. Serve with ③ as desired.

■ Cooked in the pig's feet soup, the Vietnamese rice noodles become very soft and delicious -- very suitable for the elderly or young children.

牛尾、牛丸粉
BEEF BALLS AND TAIL ON NOODLES

牛肉丸⋯⋯⋯⋯⋯⋯⋯8 個

① 牛高湯⋯⋯⋯⋯⋯⋯⋯5 杯
煮熟牛尾 [見 9 頁牛高湯]⋯⋯⋯⋯⋯⋯⋯12 兩 [450 公克]

② 魚露⋯⋯⋯⋯⋯⋯⋯1 大匙
鹽⋯⋯¾ 小匙，糖⋯⋯⋯2 小匙

③ 蔥花⋯⋯2 大匙，洋蔥⋯⋯⋯4 片

新鮮細河粉 [圖 2]⋯6 兩 [225 公克]
香草葉及蔬菜 [見 13 頁]

8 beef balls

① **5c. beef stock**
1 lb. (450g) cooked ox tail (see p. 9, beef stock)

② **1 T. fish sauce**
¾ t. salt, 2 t. sugar

③ **2 T. chopped green onions**
4 onion slices

½ lb. (225g) fresh thin rice noodles (Fig. 2)
fragrant spices/herbs and vegetables (p. 13)

1 河粉在滾水內川燙撈出，分盛 2 碗上置 ③ 料。

2 將 ①、② 料及牛肉丸燒開後加到河粉內，食時加 "香草菜及蔬菜"，可與拌醋的洋蔥片配食。

熟牛肉粉 熬高湯時可加牛腩、牛百葉或牛筋等，切片置粉上淋入 "牛高湯"。

生牛肉粉 生的薄牛肉片置粉上，加入煮滾的 "牛高湯"。

1 Blanch thin rice noodles in boiling water, drain, and separate into 2 bowls. Place ③ on top of rice noodles.

2 Bring to boil ①, ②, and beef balls, then add to thin rice noodles. Serve with "fragrant spices/herbs and vegetables". May serve with onion slices mixed with vinegar.

Rice Noodles with Cooked Beef When preparing beef stock, may add beef tenderloin, beef tripe, or beef tendon. Slice any of the above and place on cooked fresh thin rice noodles; add beef stock and serve.

Rice Noodles with Rare Beef Place thin slices of lean raw beef on cooked fresh rice noodles, add boiling beef stock and serve.

香螺檬
PERIWINKLE ON RICE NOODLES

①	高湯 [見 9 頁] 5 杯，酸子 ··1 大匙
②	番茄 [切塊]·········6 兩 [225 公克] 鹽·········¾ 小匙，糖 ·······2 小匙 魚露·········2 大匙
	檬·········6 兩 [225 公克]
③	熟香螺 [冷凍] 1 杯，炸豆腐···4 塊
	蔥 [斜切片]·········4 片
④	香草葉及蔬菜 [見 13 頁]

1 將 ① 料燒開，過濾去除酸子渣後 ，加入 ② 料煮開，見番茄熟軟待用。

2 檬煮熟 [見 10 頁]，分盛 2 碗，上置燙熱的 ③ 料及蔥，加入煮好的湯料，食時加 ④ 料。

■ 香螺不能煮過久，在湯內燙一下即可，以免過老。

①	5 c. stock (p. 9), 1 T. tamarind
②	½ lb. (225g) tomato, cut in pieces ¾ t. salt 2 t. sugar, 2 T. fish sauce
	½ lb. (225g) rice noodles
③	1 c. frozen periwinkle meat 4 pieces fried tofu
	4 green onion slices
④	fragrant spices/herbs and vegetables (p. 13)

1 Bring ① to boil, strain and discard tamarind pulp, add ② and bring to boil. Set aside when tomato is softened.

2 Cook rice noodles until done (p.10), separate into 2 bowls, top with cooked ingredients in ③ and green onion slices. Add cooked soup. Add ④ while serving.

■ Do not overcook periwinkle meat; blanch quickly in boiling soup.

番茄蛋檬
EGG AND TOMATO RICE NOODLE SOUP

	蛋·········2 個，豬絞肉·······1/2 杯
	檬·········6 兩 [225 公克]
①	蒜末·······1 小匙，蝦米·······2 大匙 番茄 [切塊]·········6 兩 [225 公克]
②	高湯 [見 9 頁] ·········5 杯 魚露·········2 大匙，鹽·······¾ 小匙
	蔥花·········1 大匙
③	香草葉及蔬菜 [見 13 頁] 空心菜莖 *[圖 1]·········隨意

1 蛋打 2 分鐘至起細泡，分次加入絞肉內至全部攪拌均勻；檬煮熟 [見 10 頁]，分盛 2 碗。

2 油 2 大匙燒熱，將 ① 料依序放入炒香，隨入 ② 料煮滾，見番茄熟軟，隨即將備好的蛋肉徐徐加入湯內，不要攪動，不要讓湯大滾以免蛋及肉分散。以中火煮開後即倒入檬內，上加蔥花，食時加 ③ 料。

★ 空心菜莖刨絲後泡水。

番茄蟹蛋檬 加入適量的蟹肉、蟹黃，即成另一種鮮味湯檬。

	2 eggs, ½ c. ground pork ½ lb. (225g) thinnest rice noodles
①	1 t. minced garlic 2 T. dried shrimp ½ lb. (225g) tomato, cut in pieces
②	5 c. stock (p. 9), ¾ t. salt 2 T. fish sauce
	1 T. chopped green onion
③	fragrant spices/herbs and vegetables (p. 13) on-choy stems* (Fig. 1) as desired

1 Beat eggs 2 minutes until frothy, gradually mix small portions into ground pork until all of the eggs are thoroughly mixed with the ground pork. Cook thinnest rice noodles until done (p.10). Separate into two bowls.

2 Heat 2 T. oil, stir-fry ① in order until fragrant, followed by ② and bring to boil. When tomatoes are softened, add prepared egg-ground pork mixture gradually into soup. Do not stir, nor cook with high heat to avoid separation of eggs from ground pork. Bring to boil with medium heat, then pour on cooked thinnest rice noodles. Top with chopped green onion, and add ③ while serving.

★ Shred on-choy stems, then soak in water.

Egg/Tomato/Crab Rice Noodle Soup
Add desired amounts of crab meat and crab maw; this becomes another tasty variation of "rice noodle soup".

1

①	牛腱、切塊豬腳各 12 兩[450 公克]
	熟豬血 [切 6 塊]……4 兩 [150 公克] 檬……………………6 兩 [225 公克]
②	印度咖哩籽、乾辣椒粉…各 2 小匙 蒜末、蝦醬……………………各 2 大匙 大乾紅辣椒 [圖 1,去籽切碎]…2 支
③	水…………20 杯,洋蔥…………1 個 香茅[5 公分長]………………8 支
④	魚露………2 大匙,糖………1 大匙
⑤	香草葉及蔬菜 [見 13 頁]

①	1 lb. (450g) ea.: beef shank, pig's feet (cut in pieces) ⅓ lb. (150g) cooked pork blood, cut in 6 pieces ½ lb. (225g) rice noodles
②	2 t. ea.: annatto seeds, dried chili powder 2 T. minced garlic 2 large dried chili peppers (Fig. 1, seedless and minced) 2 T. shrimp paste
③	20 c. water, 1 onion 8 lemon grass sections, 2" (5cm)
④	2 T. fish sauce, 1 T. sugar
⑤	fragrant spices/herbs and vegetables (p. 13)

順化牛腱檬

2 人份・Serves 2

BEEF SHANK ON RICE NOODLES

1 將 ① 料川燙撈出;油 2 大匙燒熱, ② 料內的咖哩籽用小火炒香,變黑後即撈出,再將其他 ② 各料放入炒香,隨入 ③ 料及燙過的 ① 料大火煮開,再以中火煮至肉熟軟[豬腳煮 50 分鐘先取出,牛腱需煮 2 小時];牛腱待冷切片備用。一次煮多,剩餘的留下次食用。

2 檬煮熟[見 10 頁],分盛 2 碗。

3 豬腳及煮好的高湯 5 杯加入 ④ 料燒開,放入豬血燙熱撈出,連同肉片和豬腳擺在檬上,倒入高湯,食時加 ⑤ 料。

1 Blanch ① and drain; heat 2 T. oil, stir-fry the annatto seeds in ② over low heat until blackened; remove. Stir-fry other ingredients in ② until fragrant. Add ③ and the blanched ingredients in ①, bring to boil over high heat. Reduce heat to medium and cook until meat is done (cook pig's feet 50 minutes and remove; beef shank requires cooking for 2 hours); let beef shank cool, cut into slices and set aside. Preparing a large quantity at once allows for future use.

2 Cook rice noodles until done (p.10), separate into 2 bowls.

3 Add ④ to pig's feet and 5 c. prepared stock; bring to boil. Quick-boil cooked pork blood and remove; put pork blood, sliced beef shank, and pig's feet on rice noodles. Pour stock into bowls, add ⑤ and serve.

	豬骨 [剁塊]………2 斤 [1200 公克]
①	水…20 杯,鹹魚…12 兩[450 公克] 香茅 [切段拍碎]………………8 支
②	豬肉…………………4 兩 [150 公克] 魷魚 *………4 片,蝦仁………6 隻
	檬…6 兩 [225 公克],糖…1 大匙 韭菜 [5 公分長]……………½ 杯
③	香草葉及蔬菜 [見 13 頁]

	2 ⅔ lbs. (1200g) pork bone, cut in pieces
①	20 c. water 1 lb. (450g) preserved (mam) fish 8 lemon grass (sectioned, slightly smashed)
②	⅓ lb. (150g) pork 4 squid pieces*, 6 shelled shrimp
	½ lb. (225g) rice noodles 1 T. sugar ½ c. Chinese chives, 2" (5cm) long
③	fragrant spices/herbs and vegetables (p. 13)

鹹魚湯檬

2 人份・Serves 2

SALTY FISH ON RICE NOODLES

1 豬骨放入多量水內川燙撈出,加入 ① 料[罐頭內的鹹魚汁不要]煮開,改用中火煮 2 小時即成 "鹹魚高湯"[一次煮多,剩餘的留下次用]。 ② 料內的豬肉煮熟切片,魷魚及蝦仁燙熟備用。

2 檬煮熟[見 10 頁],分盛 2 碗,上面放燙熟的 ② 料及韭菜。

3 煮好的 "鹹魚高湯" 5 杯燒開後加糖,即倒入檬內,隨意加 ③ 料食用。

★ 魷魚切法見 43 頁"炒魷魚"做法 **1** 。

1 Blanch pork bones in plenty of boiling water, put into ① (discard preserved fish juice) and bring to boil. Reduce heat to medium and cook 2 hours to make "salty fish stock" (preparing a large quantity at once allows for future use). Cook pork in ② until done and cut into slices. Quick-boil squid and shrimp; set aside.

2 Cook rice noodles until done (p.10), separate into 2 bowls. Top with cooked ingredients in ② and Chinese chives.

3 Bring 5 c. "salty fish stock" to boil, add sugar, then pour over rice noodles. Add ③ as desired and serve.

★ See p.43 "Stir-fried Squid" procedure **1** for how to cut squid.

雞絲檬
SHREDDED CHICKEN ON RICE NOODLES

1 將 ① 料煮開放入雞胸肉，再煮開後，蓋鍋燜 15 分鐘，肉熟撈出撕成絲。

2 把 ② 料拌勻煎成蛋皮切絲；蝦米在油中炒香。

3 檬煮熟[見 10 頁]，分盛 2 碗，加入豆芽菜、雞絲、蛋絲、扎肉絲、蝦米末及 ③ 料[可隨意另加紅蘿蔔絲、木耳絲等]。倒入燒滾的 ① 料即成。

■ 這是一道清淡的湯檬，煮高湯時如加入烤過的魷魚一起熬，則味道較為鮮美。吃時加 1-2 滴"桂花蟬油"，味道會比較香濃。

扎肉 [或火腿] [切絲] ·············4 片
雞胸肉·················4 兩 [150 公克]

① 高湯 [見 9 頁] ··5 杯，魚露····2 大匙
　 鹽·········¾ 小匙，糖·········2 小匙

② 雞蛋·········1 個，魚露·······¼ 小匙

蝦米 [剁碎]·······················2 大匙
檬··6 兩 [225 公克]，豆芽菜···2 杯

③ 蔥花 1 大匙，炸香紅蔥頭····½ 小匙

4 slices of pork meat loaf (or ham), shredded
⅓ lb. (150g) boneless chicken breast

① **5 c. stock (p. 9), 2 T. fish sauce**
¾ t. salt, 2 t. sugar

② **1 egg, ¼ t. fish sauce**

2 T. minced dried shrimp
½ lb. (225g) rice noodles
2 c. bean sprouts

③ **1 T. chopped green onion**
½ t. fried shallots

---

1 Bring ① to boil, add chicken breast, bring to boil again. Cover and simmer 15 minutes. When chicken is cooked, remove and shred.

2 Mix ② well, pan-fry to make a thin egg skin, slice into shreds; stir-fry dried shrimp in oil until fragrant.

3 Cook rice noodles until done (p.10), separate into 2 bowls, top with bean sprouts, shredded chicken, shredded egg, shredded meat loaf, minced dried shrimp and ③ (may also add shredded carrots, shredded wood ears, etc. as desired). Add boiling ① and serve.

■ This is a light and refreshing rice noodle soup. When preparing stock, adding baked squid enhances the stock's flavor. Add 1 to 2 drops of "mangdana essence" to further enliven the flavor of this dish.

鴨筍檬
DUCK AND BAMBOO ON RICE NOODLES

1 筍乾泡軟[最少 4 小時]，撈出切成段，水煮 30 分鐘，再泡水一天以上，使其膨脹為二倍；① 料抹在鴨表面醃 1 小時；② 料調好當沾料用。

2 將 ③ 料煮開，放入筍煮 5 分鐘，再入鴨[湯汁要滿過鴨]燒滾，煮 20 分鐘後蓋鍋燜 20 分鐘，鴨取出待冷切塊[剩餘材料留下次用；筍乾宜在鴨湯內浸泡隔夜，會更入味產生爽脆的口感]。

3 檬煮熟[見 10 頁]，分盛 2 碗。鴨塊置上。

4 取煮好的鴨湯 5 杯及適量的筍加 ④ 料煮開，湯及筍加在檬上，與高麗菜配食，鴨肉沾沾料。

鴨 ½ 隻 ·················1 斤 [600 公克]

① 鹽 ··········1 小匙，蔥········1 大匙

筍乾 [圖 1] ·····················¾ 杯

② 薑 [磨碎]、蒜末········各 1 小匙
　 魚露、糖·················各 2 小匙

③ 罐頭雞湯····2 杯，水·········15 杯

④ 魚露·······2 大匙，糖··········2 小匙
　 鹽······················¾ 小匙

檬··6 兩 [225 公克]，高麗菜絲···2 杯

½ duck, 1 ⅓ lbs. (600g)

① **1 t. salt, 1 T. green onion**

¾ c. dried bamboo shoots (Fig. 1)

② **1 t. minced ginger root**
1 t. minced garlic
2 t. fish sauce, 2 t. sugar

③ **2 c. chicken broth, 15 c. water**

④ **2 T. fish sauce**
2 t. sugar, ¾ t. salt

½ lb. (225g) rice noodles
2 c. shredded cabbage

---

1 Soak dried bamboo shoots until softened (at least 4 hours), drain and cut into sections, cook in water 30 minutes. Continue to soak in water for more than one day; yields more than double its original proportion. Rub ① on duck and marinate 1 hour; mix ② and set aside for dipping.

2 Bring ③ to boil, add bamboo shoots and cook 5 minutes. Add duck (ensure that broth covers duck), bring to boil, and cook 20 minutes. Cover and simmer 20 more minutes, remove duck and let cool, then cut into pieces (save remainder for future use; may soak dried bamboo shoots in duck soup overnight, yielding an even more delicious flavor and crispy effect).

3 Cook rice noodles until done (p.10), separate into 2 bowls, top with pieces of duck.

4 Bring to boil 5 c. duck stock, desired amounts of bamboo shoots and ④. Add soup and bamboo shoots to rice noodles, and serve with shredded cabbage. Dip duck in sauce, serve.

1

越式煎餅
VIETNAMESE PANCAKES

1 洋蔥 [8 片] .... 小半個
　蝦 [去殼] .... 12 隻

2 豬或雞肉 .... 4 兩 [150 公克]
　去皮綠豆蒸熟 [見 8 頁] ...... 3 大匙
　蕃茄 [8 片] .... 小半個

3 煎餅粉 [圖 1] .... 4 兩 [150 公克]
　黃薑粉 [或咖喱粉] .... ½ 小匙
　椰奶或鮮奶 .... ¾ 杯
　水 .... 1 杯
　油 .... 1 小匙

　豆芽菜 .... 4 杯
　甜酸辣魚露沾料或其他沾料
　[見 13 頁] .... 適量

1 將 2 料內的肉煮熟切片。

2 不黏鍋放入 2 小匙的油燒熱，先放 ¼ 的 1 料，再依序入 ¼ 的 2 各料，並加入 ½ 杯拌勻的 3 料，如同煎蛋皮，轉動鍋子使成 1 大片薄餅。

3 再改用中火煎至餅邊略蹺起，隨即放入 1 杯豆芽菜蓋鍋 1 分鐘，打開鍋蓋續煎至餅底呈焦黃色皮脆，用鍋鏟輕輕地由一邊折半，鏟出上碟，可煎 4 大片。淋入沾料非常可口，適用於早餐或便餐。

■ 趁熱吃才能吃到"煎餅'酥脆的特色。如配上"香草葉"及生菜或小芥菜[生吃]，更可以達到營養均衡的效果。

■ 傳統上餅內使用帶殼蝦及去皮綠豆。餅內的材料可隨意用炒熟絞肉或其他肉類，蔬菜類可用草菇、毛菇、高麗菜、芹菜、豆干、豆腐，紅蘿蔔或全素。

■ 煎餅粉可用粘米粉及玉米粉以 4：1 的比例混合取代。

1 ½ small onion, cut in 8 slices
1 12 shelled shrimp

2 ⅓ lb. (150g) pork or
　chicken meat
2 3 T. steamed peeled mung
　beans (p. 8)
　½ small tomato, cut in 8 slices

3 ⅓ lb. (150g) prepared flour
　(Fig. 1)
　½ t. turmeric powder or curry
　powder
　¾ c. coconut milk or milk
　1 c. water
　1 t. oil

　4 c. bean sprouts
　sweet/sour/spicy fish sauce or
　other dipping sauces (p. 13)
　as desired

1 Cook the meat or chicken in ingredient 2 and cut into slices.

2 Heat 2 t. oil in non-stick pan, add ¼ of 1, followed by ¼ of each item in 2, and add ½ c. well-mixed 3, and pan-fry to make a large, thin pancake. Agitate the pan while cooking.

3 Reduce heat to medium and pan-fry until the edge curls slightly, followed by 1 c. bean sprouts, and cover 1 minute. Remove lid of pan, continue to pan-fry until the underside of pancake is golden brown and crispy. Use spatula to slide under pancake and gently fold in half, remove and put on a plate. Makes 4 large pancakes. Drizzle with sauce. They are very tasty, and suitable for breakfast or a fast meal.

■ Serve while it's hot to enjoy the crispy and tasty quality of these pancakes. Add "fragrant spices/herbs" and lettuce or baby mustard greens (raw) for a nutritionally balanced meal.

■ Traditionally, these pancakes are served with unpeeled shrimp and peeled mung beans. Other ingredients in pancakes may include stir-fried ground pork or other meats; vegetables may include straw mushrooms, mushrooms, cabbage, celery, savory bean curd, tofu, and carrots; or create an all vegetarian pancake.

■ Instead of using prepared flour, may substitute with a mixture of rice flour and cornstarch at a 4:1 ratio.

越式春捲
VIETNAMESE EGG ROLLS

1	瘦豬絞肉.................8 兩 [300 公克] 蟹肉........½ 杯，蠔油........2 大匙 鹽........¼ 小匙，油........1 小匙
2	芋頭絲....1 杯，洋蔥 [切碎]....½ 杯 泡軟冬粉 [切小段]................½ 杯
3	水、可口可樂................各 1 杯 蘇打粉................¼ 小匙

炸油........適量，米紙 [小]....24 張
甜酸辣魚露沾料 [見 13 頁]......適量

1 將 1 料攪拌均勻，再加 2 料翻拌即為餡，分成 24 份。

2 調勻的 3 料備於深盤內，取 1 張米紙沾 3 料，平放盤內置 5 分鐘，待米紙軟表面水乾，放入 1 份餡包成春捲，共可做 24 個。[米紙做法詳見 10 頁]

3 炸油燒熱，入春捲，油溫保持中溫，邊翻邊炸 3 分鐘至表面呈金黃色酥脆。可當前菜，其他食法見 59 頁。

■ 可口可樂有加深表面顏色的效果，蘇打粉可防止炸時米紙互相黏住。

1	⅔ lb. (300g) lean ground pork ½ c. crab meat, ¼ t. salt 2 T. oyster oil, 1 t. oil
2	1 c. shredded taro root ½ c. minced onion ½ c. presoftened bean threads, cut in small sections
3	1 c. ea.: water, cola ¼ t. baking soda

24 small rice papers

oil for deep-frying
sweet/sour/spicy fish sauce
   (p. 13) as desired

1 Mix 1 thoroughly, add 2, and mix well to make filling. Divide into 24 portions.

2 Mix 3 well and set aside in a deep dish. Dip one sheet of rice paper in 3, place flat on a plate for 5 minutes until rice paper softens and surface is dry, wrap one portion of filling and roll into an egg roll. Makes 24 total (see p.10 for how to soak rice paper).

3 Heat oil for deep-frying, add egg rolls and maintain oil temperature at medium heat. Turn over and fry 3 minutes until both sides are golden brown and crispy. May be served as an appetizer. See p.59 for additional serving suggestions.

■ The cola used in 3 has a darkening effect on the egg rolls. Use baking soda to prevent rice papers from sticking to each other.

炸南瓜餅
PUMPKIN TURNOVERS

豬絞肉.....................4 兩 [150 公克]
南瓜 [或芋頭]........12 兩 [450 公克]

1	蒜末................1 小匙 洋蔥 [切碎]................2 大匙

魚露........1 大匙，春捲皮........9 張
蛋黃............1 個，炸油..........適量

1 南瓜去籽 [不需去皮]，蒸 20 分鐘至熟軟，取淨重 8 兩 [300 公克] 壓成泥。南瓜泥若太軟，可加玉米粉或用 2 張春捲皮來包。

2 油 1 大匙燒熱，將 1 料炒香，隨入絞肉炒開至熟，加魚露炒拌均勻，鏟出與南瓜泥拌勻即成餡料。春捲皮包入餡料成南瓜餅＊，炸呈金黃色酥脆即成。

★ 南瓜餅包法：春捲皮切半成 2 張三角形。A 角往上折 (圖 1)。B 角順斜邊折上，將餡裝入灰網部位 (圖 2)。D 邊貼上 E 邊上，使有餡的部分成三角形，露出的 C 角向有餡三角邊繞著繼續折，最後的 C 角用蛋黃黏住成三角形 (圖 3)。

⅓ lb. (150g) ground pork
1 lb. (450g) pumpkin
   (or taro root)

1	1 t. minced garlic 2 T. minced onion

1 T. fish sauce
9 egg roll skins
1 egg yolk, oil for deep-frying

1 Remove seeds from pumpkin (do not peel), steam 20 minutes until softened, net weight ⅔ lb. (300g), mash into paste. If the pumpkin paste is too watery, add cornstarch or wrap with two egg roll skins.

2 Heat 1 T. oil, stir-fry 1 until fragrant, followed by ground pork, stir-fry until cooked. Add fish sauce, mix well, remove from pan and mix thoroughly with pumpkin paste to make filling. Wrap the skin with filling* then deep-fry until golden and crispy. Serve.

★ To wrap the filling: Cut each egg roll skin diagonally to make two triangles. Fold angle **A** upward (Fig.1). Take angle **B** and fold to the right following the top straight edge. Fill the "gray" area with filling (Fig.2). Fold **E** edge to **D** edge so that the part with filling forms a triangle. Continue folding angle **C** toward the triangle with the filling. Moisten the **C** edge with egg yolk and seal the triangle (Fig.3).

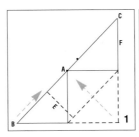
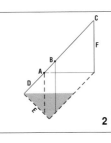
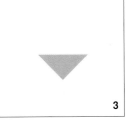

蝦米肉紙捲
MEAT AND SHRIMP RICE ROLLS

1 水燒開，分別將 ① 料煮熟撈出，湯汁保留做其他用途；蝦去殼片開，共有 16 片；肉切片，檬煮熟[見 10 頁]，備用。

2 泡軟米紙[見 10 頁]置於盤內，先放煮熟 ① 料再放生菜、檬、香草葉，由邊捲緊，中途放入韭菜露出一段，包成春捲狀；共做 4 捲，沾沾料食用。

■ 此為一道清淡不油的菜餚，可當前菜、點心或便餐。包時如將蝦置於最底下，透過米紙，呈現蝦的鮮紅及部份蔬菜的翠綠，可刺激炎炎夏日的食慾。

肉絲豬皮捲

1 豬肉 8 兩[300 公克]切 1 公分厚，抹上鹽、蒜末各 1 小匙，用油煎至兩面呈金黃色，蓋鍋燜 2 分鐘至肉熟，待冷切絲。

2 冷凍豬皮絲切 2.5 公分長略洗，放入熱水內燙 2 分鐘[水不要滾以免縮小]，略沖冷水，握乾水份，加入豬肉絲及"炒米碎粉"[見 12 頁]3 大匙拌勻，即成"肉絲豬皮"[圖 1]。以"肉絲豬皮"取代 ① 料，其他材料及做法如上。

---

① 蝦 ⋯⋯⋯⋯⋯⋯⋯⋯8 隻
豬肉 [雞或牛肉]⋯⋯4 兩 [150 公克]

米紙 [大] ⋯⋯⋯⋯⋯⋯⋯4 張
檬 ⋯⋯⋯⋯⋯⋯⋯1½ 兩 [50 公克]
生菜 ⋯⋯⋯⋯⋯⋯⋯⋯⋯4 片
香草葉 ⋯⋯⋯⋯⋯⋯⋯⋯16 片
韭菜 [15 公分] ⋯⋯⋯⋯⋯⋯8 支
海鮮醬調味沾料或其他沾料
[見 13 頁]⋯⋯⋯⋯⋯⋯⋯適量

① 8 shrimp
⅛ lb. (150g) pork, beef or chicken meat

4 large rice papers
1 ¾ oz. (50g) rice noodles
4 lettuce leaves
16 leaves of fragrant spices/herbs
8 Chinese chives, 6" (15cm) long
seasoned hoisin sauce or other dipping sauce (p. 13) as desired.

1 Boil water, separately cook ① until done, then remove. Set aside broth; peel shrimp and butterfly, totaling 16 slices; cut meat into slices, cook rice noodles until done (p.10), set aside.

2 Soak rice paper until softened (p.10) and place on a plate. Top with cooked ingredients ①, then add lettuce, rice noodles, fragrant spices/herbs, and roll tightly from one edge to the middle. Add Chinese chives, leaving a section sticking out, wrap like an egg roll; makes 4 rolls; serve with sauce.

■ This is a light and refreshing, oil-free dish; suitable as an appetizer, snack, or fast meal. When wrapping, place the pink colored shrimp at the bottom so that the reddish hue is contrasted with the lush green of the vegetables. This colorful and tasty dish is appetizing during the hot summer season.

Pork and Skin Rice Rolls

1 Cut ⅔ lb. (300g) pork to ½ inch (1cm) thickness, rub 1 t. each salt and minced garlic. Pan-fry until both sides are golden brown, cover and simmer 2 minutes until pork is done. Let cool and shred.

2 Cut frozen pork skin shreds to 1 inch (2.5cm) length, briefly wash, then cook in hot water 2 minutes (do not use boiling water to prevent shrinking). Rinse in cold water, squeeze dry, add to shredded pork and mix thoroughly with 3 T. "roasted rice powder" (p.12); the mixture becomes "shredded pork and pork skin" (Fig.1). Use "shredded pork and pork skin" instead of ①; all other ingredients and procedures are the same as above.

1

越式潤餅
VIETNAMESE SPRING ROLLS

1 油 2 大匙燒熱，炒香蒜末，再將涼薯略炒，燜煮至透明[有很多湯汁時撈出涼薯，其湯汁可當做潤餅的沾料]。

2 米紙泡軟[見 10 頁]，放入 3 片九層塔、2 片香腸、1 大匙蛋皮絲、少許碎花生及蝦米，再放入 2 大匙涼薯，在米紙內塗上少許海鮮醬及辣椒醬，捲起即可食用。

★ 即沙葛，可用白蘿蔔切絲取代。

涼薯 *[切絲] ⋯⋯⋯12 兩 [450 公克]
蒜末⋯⋯⋯1 小匙，九層塔⋯⋯30 片
香腸 [煮熟切片]⋯⋯⋯⋯⋯⋯2 條
蛋 [煎蛋皮切絲]⋯⋯⋯⋯⋯⋯2 個
碎花生、蝦米 [炸香]⋯⋯⋯各 ¼ 杯
米紙 [中] ⋯⋯⋯⋯⋯⋯⋯⋯10 張
海鮮醬、辣椒醬 ⋯⋯⋯⋯各 1 大匙

1 lb. (450g) yimaca or white radish, shredded
1 t. minced garlic
30 fresh basil leaves
2 cooked sausages, sliced
2 eggs (beaten, fried and shredded)
¼ c. ground roasted peanuts
¼ c. fried dried shrimp
10 medium rice papers
1 T. hoisin sauce
1 T. chili paste

1 Heat 2 T. oil, stir-fry minced garlic until fragrant, add yimaca then stir-fry lightly. Cover and simmer until yimaca is translucent (when lots of juice is released, remove yimaca, and set aside juice for use as a sauce).

2 Soak rice paper until softened (p.10), add 3 basil leaves, 2 slices of sausage, 1 T. shredded fried eggs, some ground roasted peanuts and fried dried shrimp, add 2 T. yimaca. Spread some hoisin sauce and chili paste on the inside of rice paper, roll and serve.

肉粉捲
MEAT IN RICE ROLLS

① 肉捲粉 * [圖 1]……4 兩 [150 公克]
水 ……………………………………2 杯
油 ……………………………………1 大匙

② 雞或豬肉 [切丁或絞肉]………⅔ 杯
蝦仁 [切碎] ………………………½ 杯
玉米粉 …………………………2 小匙

③ 蒜末 ……………………………1 小匙
洋蔥 [切碎] ………………………½ 杯
木耳 [切碎] ………………………¼ 杯

魚露 ……………………………2 小匙
甜酸辣魚露沾料 [見 13 頁]…..適量

1 將 ①、② 料分別拌勻，置 20 分鐘備用。

2 油 2 大匙燒熱，將 ③ 料依序放入炒香，隨入拌勻的 ② 料炒開，再加魚露炒拌均勻，盛起當餡料 [餡內多加入香菜及紅椒絲可增加色彩]。

3 小型不黏鍋燒熱，用紙巾沾油抹鍋後，放入 2 大匙調勻的 ① 料，轉動鍋子使成圓形，蓋鍋約 2 秒鐘，即成粉皮，取出置於盤內。

4 粉皮內放入 2 大匙的餡料，包成春捲狀，可做 16 捲；趁熱淋上 "甜酸辣魚露沾料" 食用。

★ 可用粘米粉和玉米粉以 4:1 的比例混合取代肉捲粉。

■ 此道菜可當早、午餐、便餐或前菜，喜歡吃肉的人，可配上切片的 "扎肉" [見 29 頁]，或可隨意加香菜、豆芽菜、炸香紅蔥頭等配食。

① ⅛ lb. (150g) steamed rice rolls flour* (Fig. 1)
2 c. water
1 T. oil

② ⅔ c. chicken or pork (diced or ground)
½ c. shelled shrimp, chopped
2 t. cornstarch

③ 1 t. minced garlic
½ c. minced onion
¼ c. presoftened dried wood ears, minced

2 t. fish sauce
sweet/sour/spicy fish sauce (p. 13) as desired

1 Separately mix ① then ② well, set aside 20 minutes.

2 Heat 2 T. oil, stir-fry in order each ingredient of ③ until fragrant, followed by well-mixed ② and stir-fry, add fish sauce and stir-fry, mix well, remove and set aside as filling (add coriander and shredded red chili pepper to enhance color of filling).

3 Heat small non-stick pan, grease pan with paper towel dipped in oil, add 2 T. well-mixed ①, gently turn the pan to create a circle. Cover 2 seconds and the rice roll skin is done, remove and put on a plate.

4 Put 2 T. filling onto rice roll skin, wrap like an egg roll; makes 16 rolls. Serve while hot and drizzle "sweet/sour/spicy fish sauce".

★ Instead of using steamed rice rolls flour, may use a mixture of rice flour and cornstarch at a 4:1 ratio.

■ This dish may be served as breakfast, lunch, snack, or appetizer. For those who favor meat, may also add sliced "Vietnamese ham" (p.29) or as desired, add coriander, bean sprouts, stir-fried shallots, etc.

越式砵仔糕
VIETNAMESE DISH CAKE

去皮綠豆蒸熟 [見 8 頁] ....1 杯
1 水 ....4 杯
越式砵仔糕粉 ....4 兩 [150 公克]

2 蝦米 [剁碎炒香] ....1 杯
油蔥 [見 12 頁] ....¼ 杯
炸香紅蔥頭 [見 12 頁] ....¼ 杯

小碟 [直徑 4 公分] ....16 個
甜酸辣魚露沾料 [見 13 頁].......適量

1 c. steamed peeled mung beans (p. 8)

1 4 c. water
   ⅓ lb. (150g) steamed rice cake flour

2 1 c. dried shrimp (minced and stir-
      fried)
   ¼ c. fried green onions (p. 12)
   ¼ c. fried shallots (p. 12)

16 small dishes (diameter 1½", 4cm)
sweet/sour/spicy fish sauce (p. 13)
   as desired

1 蒸熟去皮綠豆壓成泥；① 料攪勻，用中火邊煮邊攪 3 分鐘後改小火，至底部略凝固時即離火，續攪拌成糊漿。① 料內的砵仔糕粉可用粘米粉和木薯粉以 2:1 的比例調配。

2 蒸鍋水燒開，每個小碟舀入糊漿七分滿，可做成 32 個，每次 16 個放入蒸鍋內，用大火蒸 4 分鐘至透明，微溫時用刀沾水取出。

3 每個砵仔糕上放入適量的綠豆泥及 ② 料即成。微溫時食用較有彈性，吃時淋上"甜酸辣魚露沾料"。

1 Mash mung beans to paste; mix ① well, with medium heat, cook while stirring for 3 minutes, then reduce heat to low; cook until the bottom begins to harden slightly, remove from heat, and continue to stir until mixture becomes pasty. Steamed rice cake flour in ① may be substituted with a mixture of rice flour and tapioca starch at a 2:1 ratio.

2 Boil water for steam pot, fill each small dish with filling until 70% full, makes 32 dish cakes. Put 16 dishes in steam pot at one time, steam with high heat 4 minutes until cakes are translucent. Pry cakes loose with moist knife while still lukewarm.

3 Dress each cake with proper amounts of mung bean paste and ②. It's best to serve while lukewarm; drizzle with "sweet/sour/spicy fish sauce".

什錦豆冰
ASSORTED BEANS ICE SLUSH

紅、白豆、糖 ....各 1 杯
去皮綠豆蒸熟 [見 8 頁] ....1 杯

1 糖 ....1 杯，水 ....1 杯

刨冰 ....8 杯，椰奶 ....2 杯

1 c. ea.: red and white beans
1 c. sugar
1 c. steamed peeled mung beans
   (p. 8)

1 1 c. sugar, 1 c. water

8 c. shaved ice, 2 c. coconut milk

1 紅、白豆分別煮熟後各加糖 ½ 杯；① 料煮成糖水。

2 杯內放入紅、白、綠豆各 ¼ 杯、糖水 2 大匙、刨冰 1 杯及椰奶 ¼ 杯即可。

1 Separately cook red and white beans until done, add ½ c. sugar to each; cook ① to make syrup.

2 In a large glass, add ¼ c. each red, white, and mung beans, 2 T. syrup, 1 c. shaved ice, and ¼ c. coconut milk; serve.

石榴洋菜冰
AGAR ICE SLUSH

什錦豆冰 · ASSORTED BEANS ICE SLUSH
石榴洋菜冰 · AGAR ICE SLUSH

去皮綠豆蒸熟 [見 8 頁]··· ½ 杯
洋菜··· ⅛ 包，椰奶··· ¾ 杯

1 荸薺 [切小丁]5 個，食用紅色水··· 5 滴
木薯粉 [或玉米粉]··· 2 大匙

2 糖··· ¾ 杯，水··· 3 杯

1 洋菜 1 包為 42 公克，剪下 ⅛ 段加水 2 杯，煮開後用中火續煮 5 分鐘至洋菜溶化，倒入碗內，冰涼後切長方形薄片。

2 將 ① 料內的荸薺丁拌入紅色水再加木薯粉攪勻，在滾水內略燙，撈起過冷水 [可重覆以上各步驟，以增加口感]。

3 ② 料煮開成糖水，冰涼後再加蒸熟綠豆、洋菜凍、紅色馬蹄粒及椰奶即成。

½ c. steamed peeled
   mung beans (p. 8)
⅛ package of agar
¾ c. coconut milk

1 5 water chestnuts, diced
   5 drops of red coloring
   2 T. tapioca starch or cornstarch

2 ¾ c. sugar, 3 c. water

1 One package of agar is 1 ½ oz. (42g), cut a ⅛ section and add to 2 c. water, bring to boil. Reduce heat to medium and continue cooking 5 minutes until agar is melted. Pour into a bowl, chill, then cut into thin rectangular slices.

2 Mix the water chestnuts in ① with red coloring, then mix well with tapioca starch. Quick-boil in boiling water, remove, and rinse with cold water (may repeat above procedures to make chewy).

3 Bring ② to boil, which becomes syrup, let cool then chill. Add steamed peeled mung beans, chilled agar slices, red water chestnuts, and coconut milk. This is a refreshing dessert for the summer season.

西米露甜湯
TAPIOCA PEARLS DESSERT SOUP

西米 [圖 1] ·························¼ 杯

1｜南瓜、木薯·切塊 12 兩 [450 公克]
水 ·····························4 杯

海帶絲 [圖 2，泡過水] ·······1 杯
糖 ·····························¾ 杯
椰漿 [見 8 頁] ···············¾ 杯

¼ c. tapioca pearls (Fig. 1)

1. lb. (450g) pumpkin and
   tapioca, cut in pieces
4 c. water

1 c. shredded seaweed
   (Fig. 2, presoftened)
¾ c. sugar
¾ c. thick coconut milk (p. 8)

1 將 ① 料煮開，改中火煮 10 分鐘，待南瓜及木薯熟軟後，加入海帶再煮開，去除泡沫，續加糖煮至溶化，倒入椰漿即刻熄火。

2 水 2 杯煮開，入西米煮滾後，改中火續煮 4 分鐘 [中途需攪拌] 至透明狀撈出，倒入煮好的南瓜甜湯中，冷熱食均可。

■ 西米不能煮太爛，只要外層呈透明狀即可撈出，待泡入糖水中即會吸水而透明；甜湯內的材料，可隨喜好加芋頭、蓮子、去皮花生、紅棗 [去籽]、或香蘭葉等。

粿條甜湯 用美荻粿條 [見 11 頁] 代替西米，其他材料及做法同上。

1 Bring ① to boil, reduce heat to medium and cook 10 minutes until pumpkin and tapioca soften. Add shredded seaweed and bring to boil, remove suds, followed by sugar, and cook until it melts. Add thick coconut milk and immediately turn off heat.

2 Bring 2 c. water to boil, add tapioca pearls and bring to boil again. Reduce heat to medium and cook 4 minutes (stir occasionally) until tapioca pearls appear translucent, remove and pour into the cooked pumpkin sweet soup. Serve cold or hot.

■ Do not overcook tapioca pearls. Remove as soon as the surface appears translucent. Once soaked in syrup, they will absorb it and become entirely translucent. The ingredients of the sweet soup may vary as desired: may add taro root, lotus seeds, peeled peanuts, red dates (pitted), or pandan leaves.

Sweet Tapioca Sticks Soup Use tapioca sticks (p.11) instead of tapioca pearls. Other ingredients and cooking procedures are the same as above

綠豆爽
MUNG BEAN SOUP

1｜去皮綠豆蒸熟 [見 8 頁] ·········2 杯
糖 ····1 杯，水 ···········4 杯
澄麵 [或玉米粉] ···········5 大匙

椰漿 [見 8 頁] ···············½ 杯

2 c. steamed peeled mung
   beans (p. 8)
1｜1 c. sugar, 4 c. water
5 T. wheat starch (or
   cornstarch)

½ c. thick coconut milk (p. 8)

1 將 ① 料攪拌煮開成透明狀，食時酌量淋入椰漿。綠豆爽可當飯後甜點，冷或熱食均可。

■ 依個人喜好加入香蘭葉或香草精。

1 Bring ① to boil and stir until it becomes translucent. Add desired amount of thick coconut milk while serving. This dish may be served as a dessert, delicious cold or hot.

■ As desired, add pandan leaves or vanilla extract.

眉豆糯米粥

SWEET BEAN PORRIDGE

眉豆 [圖 1] ·······························1 杯
糯米 ·······································¾ 杯

① 糖 ·······································¾ 杯
香蘭葉 [5 公分長] ···················8 片
或香草精 ·························¼ 小匙

椰漿 [見 8 頁] ·······················½ 杯

1 眉豆泡水隔夜，重新加水 3 杯燒開，用中火煮 20 分鐘至豆熟軟，汁收乾時熄火，取出略沖水，去掉豆皮瀝乾備用[即 2 杯] [可買現成罐裝眉豆]。

2 糯米泡水 30 分鐘，重新加水 5 杯煮 10 分鐘至米熟，隨即放入眉豆，煮時需隨時攪動以防焦底，最後加 ① 料煮開至糖溶化即熄火，食時酌量加入椰漿，趁熱食用。

■ 糯米的黏性比一般米高，不必用玉米粉勾芡，照份量做好，等 20 分鐘後即成濃稠狀。可做早餐或飯後甜品。

芋頭糯米粥 芋頭切塊[2 杯]，蒸熟後代替眉豆。其他材料與做法與眉豆糯米粥同。亦可用玉米及南瓜取代。

1 c. black eyed beans (Fig. 1)
¾ c. glutinous rice

① ¾ c. sugar
8 pandan leaves (2", 5cm)
   or ¼ t. vanilla extract

½ c. thick coconut milk (p. 8)

1 Soak black eyed beans overnight, discard water then add 3 c. water, bring to boil. Cook with medium heat 20 minutes until beans soften, turn off heat when water evaporates. Remove and rinse in water, peel beans, drain, and set aside (about 2 c.). May purchase canned prepared black eyed beans.

2 Soak glutinous rice in water 30 minutes, discard water then add 5 c. water, cook 10 minutes until rice is done. Add black eyed beans, stir constantly to prevent burning at the bottom. Add ① and bring to boil until sugar melts, immediately turn off heat. Serve hot with desired amount of thick coconut milk.

■ Glutinous rice is stickier than regular rice; therefore, cornstarch is not needed to thicken. Cook prescribed portion, set aside 20 minutes and the rice becomes thick and pasty. May serve this dish as breakfast or dessert.

Sweet Taro Root Porridge Cut taro root into pieces (2 c.), steam until done and use instead of black eyed beans. Other ingredients and cooking procedures are the same as "sweet bean porridge". May also substitute with corn and pumpkin.

糯米飯
STEAMED GLUTINOUS RICE

尖糯米 ·······················1 杯	

1
| 糖 ·····························⅓ 小匙 |
| 鹽 ·····························⅛ 小匙 |
| 椰奶 ···························8 大匙 |

2
| 糖 ·····························3 大匙 |
| 鹽 ·····························¾ 小匙 |
| 椰奶 ···························7 大匙 |

竹籠*[圖 1]·····················1 組

★ 專門用來蒸糯米飯的竹籠，方便且效果佳，若無竹籠可用一般蒸籠或電鍋。

■ 糯米飯可當正餐、早點、或飯後甜點，在越南的街頭小販多用香蕉葉包裹，插上葉柄當杓子，或用手捏緊蕉葉使裏面的糯米成飯糰。

基本糯米飯

1 將糯米洗淨，泡水 6 ～ 8 小時，蒸時瀝乾水份放於竹籠內。

2 鍋內的水燒開，將竹籠置鍋上[滾水不宜觸及竹籠]，不加蓋大火蒸 10 分鐘至上面的糯米已差不多熟時，兩手握住竹籠凹形的兩邊甩動將糯米翻面[甩動時糯米若散開不成糰，表示米還生]，翻面的糯米再蒸 3 分鐘至熟透即成基本糯米飯。

椰奶糯米飯 基本糯米飯 拌入 1 料，再放回尚熱的竹籠內，不開火加蓋燜 10 分鐘即成。可捏成餅狀兩面煎黃，與烤雞食用。

一般甜糯米飯 基本糯米飯 拌入 2 料，再放回尚熱的竹籠內，不開火加蓋燜 10 分鐘即成。可配芒果當飯後甜點。

油飯 將蝦米、香菇、肉絲、香腸加調味料炒香後，加高湯 8 大匙與基本糯米飯拌勻，再放回尚熱的竹籠內，不開火加蓋燜 10 分鐘即成。

紅色甜糯米飯 泡好的糯米內加入木鱉的紅色果肉，蒸成顏色呈鮮橘紅色即成。

翠綠甜糯米飯 泡好的糯米內加入香蘭葉精，蒸成呈翠綠色並有香蘭葉的清香。

紅豆糯米飯 煮熟的紅豆與泡過水的黑糯米煮成飯，可加綠豆泥在黑糯米飯上，食時加糖。

花生糯米飯 花生連衣煮熟與泡過水的糯米一起蒸，可配上炒香的芝麻鹽。

糯玉米飯 乾的白色糯玉米粒[即去胚種的白色糯玉米粒，有罐頭出售]煮熟與糯米蒸成飯，加入綠豆泥拌勻，吃時加入炸香紅蔥頭、糖及鹽。

1 c. glutinous rice (long)

1
⅓ t. sugar, ⅛ t. salt
8 T. coconut milk

2
3 T. sugar, ¾ t. salt
7 T. coconut milk

1 bamboo basket* (Fig. 1)

★ The bamboo basket designed for steaming glutinous rice is very convenient and yields great results. If not available, use regular steam basket or electric rice cooker.

■ Steamed glutinous rice may be served as a meal or a dessert. In the back streets of Vietnam, street vendors sell this dish wrapped in banana leaves with the leaf stem as a utensil, or they squeeze the banana leaf wrap to make steamed glutinous rice balls.

Basic Steamed Glutinous rice

1 Wash glutinous rice, soak in water 6-8 hours. Drain, then put inside bamboo basket.

2 Bring water to boil for steaming, place bamboo basket on pot (boiling water should not touch bamboo basket), steam uncovered with high heat for 10 minutes. When the glutinous rice appears done, remove bamboo basket, hold two protruding sides of the basket, shake-and-flip the rice (glutinous rice that separates instead of clumping together indicates rice is still uncooked). After shaking-and-flipping the rice, replace bamboo basket on to pot and continue steaming for 3 minutes until rice is thoroughly cooked.

Coconut Rice Mix *Basic Steamed Glutinous Rice* with 1. Return the rice to the still warm bamboo basket, cover and let stand for 10 minutes. May flatten and pan-fry both sides until golden brown, serve with baked chicken.

Regular Sweet Rice Mix *Basic Steamed Glutinous Rice* with 2. Return the rice to the still warm bamboo basket, cover and let stand for 10 minutes. May serve with mango as a dessert.

Oily Rice Stir-fry dried shrimp, shredded Chinese black mushrooms, meat, sausage and seasonings, until fragrant. Mix with 8 T. stock and *Basic Steamed Glutinous Rice*. Return the rice to the still warm bamboo basket, cover and let stand for 10 minutes.

Sweet Flaming Rice Add the red flesh of trai gac fruit to soaked glutinous rice, steam to a bright orange color.

Sweet Jade Rice Add pandan leaf extract to soaked glutinous rice, steam to a light refreshing fragrance and a lush green color.

Beans and Glutinous Rice Add cooked red beans to pre-soaked black glutinous rice and steam. Steamed peeled mung bean paste may be added to steamed black glutinous rice. Add sugar when serving.

Peanuts and Glutinous Rice Add cooked unpeeled peanuts with pre-soaked glutinous rice and steam, may top with stir-fried sesame salt.

Hominy and Glutinous Rice Mix cooked hominy grits (de-stemmed hominy; sold in cans) with glutinous rice and steam, add steamed peeled mung bean paste and mix thoroughly. Add stir-fried shallots, sugar, and salt when serving.

1

甜味炸四蔬
FOUR SWEET FRIED VEGETABLES

① 炸蝦粉和蕉粉 * ....1½ 杯
椰茸 ....⅓ 杯
芝麻 ....2 大匙
糖 ....1 大匙
椰奶 ....½ 杯

水 ....½ 杯
香蕉 [或芭蕉]** 、番薯、芋頭、南
瓜 ....共 12 兩 [450 公克]
炸油 ....適量

1 將 ① 料放入容器內，慢慢加水拌成麵糊備用。調出來的麵糊濃，則炸出來的皮較厚；麵糊稀則皮較薄。

2 香蕉及其他蔬菜切成 0.7 公分厚。

3 炸油燒熱，將切好的各類蔬菜逐一沾上麵糊，放入油內，油保持中溫炸至表面凝固即可翻動，炸 5 分鐘呈金黃色酥脆即撈出。

* 買現成的"炸蝦粉和蕉粉"，炸出來的酥皮效果極佳，置 30 分鐘後，酥皮仍不變質；其成份為麵粉、玉米粉、發粉、蛋白粉。任何酥炸粉均可取代"炸蝦粉和蕉粉"。

** 不宜選過熟的香蕉或芭蕉，以免炸後過於熟軟。

① 1 ½ c. banana shrimp batter
   mix*
1 ⅓ c. coconut shreds
2 T. sesame
1 T. sugar
½ c. coconut milk

½ c. water
1 lb. (450g) total: banana**,
   yam, taro root, pumpkin
oil for deep-frying

1 Place ① into a container, slowly add water and mix well into batter; set aside. If the batter is thick, then the fried skin is thicker; a thinner batter yields a thinner skin.

2 Slice banana and other vegetables into thin slices.

3 Heat oil for deep-frying, dip all cut vegetables in batter, put into oil, maintain oil temperature at medium heat. Deep-fry until surface hardens, turn over, then fry 5 minutes until golden brown and crispy, remove.

* Use ready-made "banana shrimp batter mix" for best results; even after setting aside for 30 minutes, the fried food remains crispy. Its contents are wheat flour, cornstarch, baking powder, and powdered egg white. Any batter mix may be substituted for "banana shrimp batter mix".

** Overly ripe bananas are not suitable since they are too soft after frying.

烤甜木薯糕 1 份 · Makes 1
TAPIOCA CAKE

木薯 [見 11 頁]······1 斤 [600 公克]

1
- 蛋 [不需打散]······1 個
- 奶精······½ 杯
- 椰奶······½ 杯
- 糖······1 杯
- 鹽······⅛ 小匙
- 香草精······⅛ 小匙

奶油······1 大匙
圓烤盤 [直徑 15 公分]······1 個

1 ⅓ lbs. (600g) tapioca (p. 11)

1
- **1 egg (not beaten)**
- **½ c. half and half**
- **½ c. coconut milk**
- **1 c. sugar**
- **⅛ t. salt**
- **⅛ t. vanilla extract**

1 T. butter
round baking pan (diameter 6", 15cm)

1 木薯去皮及中間纖維莖後，取淨重 12 兩[450 公克]，刨成細絲；烤盤內放入直徑 15 公分的圓型鋁紙，以便烤後易於取出；將拌勻的 1 料及木薯絲混合成木薯糊備用。

2 烤箱預熱 400°F[200°C]，將奶油放入烤盤內，待溶化後塗抹烤盤四週。

3 將拌好的木薯糊倒入烤盤內，烤 1 小時後，用牙籤插入取出，無未熟黏液且表面呈金黃色即可取出。

■ 市面上有現成刨絲的木薯，放在冷凍櫃內出售，對繁忙者極為方便，但沒有自己新鮮刨絲的好吃。

烤鹹木薯糕 香腸[切小丁]、蝦米[剁碎炒香]各 ⅓ 杯，高湯 1 杯，蛋 1 個，蔥花、炸香紅蔥頭各 1 大匙，鹽 ½ 小匙。用以上材料取代 1 料，其他做法同上。

1 Peel tapioca and devein, net weight 1 lb. (450g), shred; place a 6 inch (15 cm) diameter round foil into baking pan so that cake is easy to remove. Combine well-mixed 1 and shredded tapioca into paste and set aside.

2 Heat oven to 400°F(200°C), use butter to grease pan.

3 Pour tapioca paste into pan, bake 1 hour; test doneness with a toothpick, remove when toothpick comes out clean and cake appears golden brown.

■ Markets sell shredded tapioca in the refrigerated section. While it is very convenient for busy people, it is not as tasty as freshly shredded tapioca.

Salty Tapioca Cake Combine ⅓ c. each: sausage (diced) and dried shrimp (minced and stir-fried); 1 c. stock, 1 egg; 1 T. each chopped green onion and fried shallots; and ½ t. salt. Use above mixture instead of 1 above; other procedures are the same as above.

香蘭葉七層糕 1 份 · Makes 1
PANDAN SEVEN LAYERED CAKE

1
- 木薯粉 [見 11 頁]······3 杯
- 糖······1⅔ 杯
- 椰奶······3¼ 杯
- 鹽······½ 小匙

香蘭葉精······¼ 小匙

2 去皮綠豆蒸熟 [見 8 頁]······¼ 杯

圓蒸盤 [直徑 18 公分]······1 個

1
- **3 c. tapioca starch (p.11)**
- **1 ⅔ c. sugar**
- **3 ¼ c. coconut milk**
- **½ t. salt**

¼ t. pandan screwpine flavored paste

2 **¼ c. steamed peeled mung beans (p. 8)**

round baking pan (diameter 7", 18cm)

1 將 1 料拌勻成無顆粒的糊狀，取 3 杯加入香蘭葉精，調勻成綠糊漿。分成四等份[每份 ¾ 杯]。

2 2 料壓成泥，與剩下的 1 料調勻成白糊漿。分成三等份[每份 1 杯]。

3 蒸鍋水燒開，蒸盤內不需塗油，放入 1 份綠糊漿，大火蒸 5 分鐘。蒸盤取出再加入 1 份白糊漿，大火蒸 10 分鐘。如此反覆地把其餘的每份材料按綠白相間的方式，每層分別以大火蒸 10 分鐘，全部蒸好後，待冷即可扣出食用。

■ 木薯粉做出來的糕點很有韌性又好吃。

1 Mix 1 thoroughly until it becomes a smooth paste. Use 3 c. of well-mixed 1, add pandan screwpine flavored paste, and mix thoroughly to make green paste, divide into 4 portions (¾ c. each).

2 Mash 2, mix with the remaining 1 to make white paste. Mix thoroughly and divide into 3 portions (1 c. each).

3 Boil water for steaming, use ungreased pan, put in 1 portion green paste, steam with high heat for 5 minutes. Remove pan and top with 1 portion white paste, steam with high heat for 10 minutes. Repeat above procedure, alternating green and white paste, until all portions of green and white paste are used; steam each additional layer with high heat for 10 minutes. After steaming all portions, let cool, and pry loose, put on a plate.

■ Cakes made with tapioca starch taste chewy and are delicious.

索引

INDEX